Keeping Bums in Seats

The NQT's Guide to Behaviour Management

Stephanie Caswell

DEDICATION

To my wonderful family, my beautiful boys and my fantastic friends. Thank you so much for your belief and support.

I've finally done it!

CONTENTS

Keeping Bums in Seats

ACKNOWLEDGMENTS

With many thanks to my editor, Kathy Carter, who polished my first draft and gave me fantastic guidance on getting this book out there in a way that would be most helpful to you all. Thanks also to Ida Sveningsson for the amazing design for my front cover.

A special thanks to my friend, editor and proof-reader, Kay Ribeiro. Quite frankly, without your endless support and belief in me, this book would never have been written. Here's to the next one… and to more brunches on a Sunday to talk through life and love.

An extra special thank you to my best friend and husband, Paul Caswell. You've listened to me talk about writing this book for the last 5 years and finally I have done it! Your support has meant I have had the courage and belief to put the words on paper and I can't thank you enough for that. I promise I won't buy any more books about writing, I think I have enough for now…

Finally, a big thank you to all of you – the NQTs who have picked up this book and read it. Without you, it would be sitting on a dusty shelf somewhere… or still be on my hard drive!

Introduction

The children are standing on the tables, pencil missiles are being launched across the room, and you're crouched in the corner in the foetal position. You're desperately trying to get your pupils to listen to you, but no sound is coming out of your mouth.

Suddenly, a table is hurled through the window and the sound of smashing glass rises above the din…

You wake up, drenched in sweat, with your heart beating so hard it feels like a pneumatic drill pumping in your chest. Burying yourself under the duvet, you realise that today is the first day of the new academic year, and in a few hours' time you're going to be opening your door to thirty eager new faces.

Sound like you? Well, fear not! *Keeping Bums in Seats* is here to give you strategies that you can use in the primary school classroom from the very first day.

More importantly, these are the strategies that work.

This book is for newly qualified teachers (NQTs) who want to get the very best out of their pupils in a calm and well-managed classroom environment. It's also for practitioners who have an open mind, a sense of humour and a willingness to try new things.

With over ten years of teaching experience in a variety of roles, including NQT mentor and deputy head, I have spoken to many teachers about what works with behaviour management and what doesn't. I have read about and tested many strategies and picked the best ones to include in this book. My aim is to give you a fresh new insight into effective behaviour management.

I promise that if you put these strategies into place, you will be able to manage your class with ease and confidence. You will feel in control and be able to concentrate on the most important things: teaching and learning. That's why we're in this job, after all! I want you to feel as though you are able to tackle any behaviour that comes your way, which will, in turn, enable you to become an outstanding teacher.

Don't be the teacher who worries about managing your class; be the teacher who appears cool, calm, and collected in a moment of perceived 'crisis'. Be the teacher who has everything under control. Be the teacher who isn't burying their head under the duvet on 1ˢᵗ September, wishing for one more day of holiday. Well, okay... maybe that's asking a little too much! In short, be the teacher you want to be.

The behaviour management strategies that you're about to read are proven to create a well-managed, calm class. All you have to do is read through each chapter carefully, think about how you can apply that particular technique to your own teaching repertoire, and begin to make a plan for implementation.

Take control of your behaviour management; make your class the best learners *they* can be and you the best teacher *you* can be. Good luck!

How to read this book

This book can be read in one of two ways. You can either read it through from beginning to end *or* dip into the sections that are most relevant to you.

Personally, I would read the whole thing through first. Then I would go back and reread the relevant chapters in more detail, making notes as I go.

Whichever way you choose to read it, the aim is for you to get lots of strategies from this book that you can use straight away with your class.

However, my books do come with a health warning: I tell it like it is. You're at the coal face (or chalk face), not sitting comfortably in a chair, reading about a hobby you have. I tell you what you need to know and will tell you when I think you need to step up to the plate.

So get stuck in and absorb the information. While you're reading, make notes of things that you want to try. I'll wait whilst you go and get your pen and paper… Go on!

CHAPTER 1

The Importance of Behaviour Management

Every school has a behaviour policy, and for good reason. Staff and parents want a consistent and well-researched approach to managing behaviour across the school. The policy should be something that is easily put in place, which all members of staff follow without question.

Your school's policy will form part of your practice, and it is important that you read it before you start your new job. Why? Simply put, you don't want to be doing something that isn't in the policy. It protects you against complaints and ensures that the children understand that wherever they are in the school, the policy applies to them.

Of course, you wouldn't present it to the children in the form of a 'policy', but perhaps as 'the school rules' or a 'behaviour ladder'. You can keep referring back to these to help you inform your own class's behaviour systems or when dealing with behaviour that might be more challenging.

While the behaviour policy should inform some of your practice, so too should a solid set of behaviour principles that influence your 'style'. Not every teacher manages behaviour in the same way, and you want to develop a way that feels right for you. If you are able to do this, then confidence naturally follows. This will then lead to a belief that you can manage any type of behaviour that comes your way; this is what we are aiming for.

What is behaviour management?

Perceptions of behaviour management vary, and teachers will approach it in very different ways.

Managing behaviour is so much more than making sure your pupils can line up quietly, complete a piece of work in the time given, and realise that getting up for the seven hundredth time to 'sharpen my pencil' isn't acceptable.

It is about creating a positive learning environment — an environment where children feel that they can take risks with their learning and make mistakes without the worry of being ridiculed by others for getting it wrong. Your classroom must be a place where the most valuable learning takes place, with a sense of respect, humour, and understanding at the heart of it.

Easy then! You may as well close the book and go and get on with it...

Still here? Good. Keep reading on and you will find that creating the type of classroom that I have mentioned above is not as daunting as you may think.

Why is behaviour management so important?

Without outstanding behaviour management, it is impossible for outstanding teaching and learning to occur.

Controversial, maybe. Fact, most definitely.

Now put away your pitchforks and your flaming torches, and listen up. Behaviour management underpins excellent classroom practice; it ensures that all children achieve. Not only that, it provides children with the three S's:

• Safety

- Security

- Sense of belonging

For some children, the school, and more importantly the people within it, will become their family, providing them with the love and care that they may not get at home.

Getting your behaviour management principles right, therefore, becomes crucial.

How to create positive behaviour management principles

Start off by using the three key principles below:

Respect

This principle has to underpin your practice, without a shadow of a doubt.

Why? Because mutual respect is the key to getting the behaviour you want out of your class and out of individual pupils.

You may think that respect only works for older children, but believe me, even our youngest children respond to a respectful approach to managing their behaviour. If nothing else, it teaches them how important respect is in society and as a social skill.

Humour

The use of humour is debated across the teaching profession, but it has served me well, and I recommend it wholeheartedly as a behaviour management approach.

Humour can diffuse a situation faster than the bomb squad and take the tension away from a potentially challenging situation. Children enjoy being taught by teachers who don't take themselves seriously all of the time. There is a time and place for being serious, and you'll know when that is; but there is also a time and a place to smile, have fun, and see the lighter side of life.

However, this principle comes with a warning: humour, yes. Taking the p*ss out of pupils, not so much.

There is a line, and it's not to be crossed.

Consistency

How many times have you tried to catch some form of public transport and it's delayed, replaced by buses, or there's been a diversion because of road works? You're not able to rely on it to get you from A to B in the same way, at the same time, each day.

Frustrating, isn't it?

Well, the same can be said for how the children in your class feel when you change your behaviour management strategies more times than you change your underwear. Order becomes chaos; the sense of belonging floats out of the window, and any thought of teaching and learning is lost into the ether.

Be consistent, or you will consistently lose control, patience, and — dare I say it — the respect of your class.

What if I am not naturally confident with behaviour management?

Not everyone feels like a superhero when welcoming a new class for the first time, and that's perfectly normal.

Behaviour management is something you will get better at with practise. Read fantastic books (like this one, of course!), observe more experienced teachers, and take advice.

I feel the need to repeat that last one: Take advice.

And don't worry about asking for it, either — have you ever met a teacher who doesn't enjoy talking about their job?

Give yourself time

When I started teaching in 2004, I was convinced that I wanted to teach in Key Stage 1 for as long as my career allowed it.

Four years and two children later (I don't hang about, you know), I found myself with the prospect of teaching Year 6 for the first time. The very thought of it made me have many a sleepless night.

I knew I would have to tackle this challenge head on and give the impression that I hadn't given it a second thought. I had to act as though managing Year 6 behaviour was something I could do with my eyes shut. I remember walking down to pick the class up from the playground, striding outside with my head held high but my heart pounding in my ears.

I've never looked back since and firmly believe that Year 6 is the year group for me. Funny what a bit of acting and courage does to your teaching skills. Give yourself time to find the year group that is right for you – it may be completely different to the one you start off in and your behaviour management style will adapt accordingly.

Mistakes

At the end of each chapter, there is a section, like this one, about mistakes that can be made when managing behaviour. Learning from your mistakes is important. It makes you a better teacher, just as it makes the children better learners. Mistakes, however, can make your teaching experience harder before it gets any easier. If you realise you're making mistakes, try to turn them around and make the choices that will be more helpful to you.

You must remember to believe in yourself. Even if this belief feels false at first, it will soon begin to feel natural. In turn, your confidence will grow and feel natural too. Your principles will become stronger and will form the basis of your practice. More importantly, you will believe in these principles and stick to them.

A common mistake is not to take that risk in the first place because you don't believe in your own ability. The first step is always the hardest but is undoubtedly the most important.

Action steps

1. Establish the kind of environment you want in your classroom and how you want the children to feel when they're working in there.

2. Consider the behaviour principles I suggested — how comfortable do you feel with these? Remember, you don't have to be a stand-up comedian, but make sure the children know that underneath your more serious exterior is a person who can have fun.

3. Do not worry if you are not naturally confident at behaviour management. You can use the tips in this book to help develop your teacher persona. My principles are at the core of my teaching and my personal values. Your own principles should be what underpin your practice – what do you feel are your principles at this point in your career?

Read on, Macduff!

The next chapter will give you insight into *why* children behave the way they do. This is important, as it can help you understand the particular actions of a child or give you a broad base on which to develop your key principles and behaviour management 'style'.

CHAPTER 2

Behaviour in Children

Children's behaviour can, quite frankly, drive you mad.

They say and do things that leave you exasperated. No matter how experienced a teacher you are, there will still be times when the behaviour choices that a child has made completely stun you. You feel yourself shaking your head and, with a heavy heart, picking up the phone to call the child's parents.

But children are children. They don't yet have the full maturity to understand why they behave in the way that they do. Some children learn to manage and control their behaviour only through direct intervention. Your job is to be a good role model for behaviour and to praise the good behaviour choices of children in your class.

Note how I said 'behaviour choices' rather than 'behaviour'. The children need to know that it is their *choice* of behaviour that you are disappointed in, not the children themselves. Remember, we are here to develop the pupils into well-rounded members of society, not to crush their spirits and self-respect.

Taking this further, there is one strategy that should *never* be in your metaphorical toolbox: shouting. Sounding disappointed, yes, but shouting? Most definitely no.

When was the last time you were shouted at? How did it make you feel? As adults, we rarely shout at other adults, but if it happens, being shouted at probably makes you feel disheartened and shaken. Why would you want to make a child feel like that?

Shouting is 'old school'. Understanding the reasons for behaviour and supporting the child appropriately is 'new school', and most definitely the only way forward.

Having said that, there is a time when shouting is acceptable and should be tolerated. That one and only time is when a child is in immediate danger. But that's it.

Glad we've cleared that one up. Let's move on.

What is behaviour?

All behaviour is communication. If you take nothing else from this book, then please take this one nugget of wisdom.

Let me simplify it even more: children behave in certain ways to try to communicate with you. Their behaviour is just their physical and emotional response to something else that is going on in their lives.

A change in behaviour is particularly significant. It can be a sign that things have changed, either at home or at school and this may need to be investigated further. This could include difficulties with friendships or problems within the family. The more you are aware of any difficulties, the more support you can provide for that child.

Behaviour can be compared to an iceberg. The 'Iceberg Model' is an extremely useful tool when considering a child's behaviour. In fact, it is useful when considering the behaviour of adults, too.

Imagine an iceberg out at sea. More often than not, teachers only see the tip of the iceberg (the behaviour) that protrudes above the waterline. The real problems that lead to the behaviour are hidden deep beneath the surface, sometimes stretching far below. A child's behavioural responses may be inextricably linked to something going on at home or at school that you are unaware of. Hidden beneath the surface could be:

- Family bereavement
- Divorce or family separation
- Eviction
- Caring for a disabled sibling or parent
- Bullying

Children might not have the language skills to tell you what is upsetting them below the visible surface of that iceberg, so it is your job to try to, sensitively, find out.

How?

By talking to the child, but also to parents, other professionals, and the staff in your school who may have worked with this child or family before. It is not your job to try to understand the situation all on your own.

Why is it important to look at the theory behind behaviour?

Understanding what may underpin a child's behaviour ensures that we deal with it in the most appropriate way.

You may have heard older generations claim that the approach to disciplining children twenty, thirty, or forty years ago was the most effective way of dealing with behaviour, and that there weren't the behaviour problems that are associated with the generation of children today.

However, our understanding of behaviour itself has grown. Through research, schools are now able to meet the needs of children in a far more helpful and appropriate way.

Gone are the cane and the 'dunce hat', and in their place is a greater sense of understanding, as well as strategies to support children in making better behaviour choices.

Confidence that you can respond effectively to a child's behaviour comes from understanding what lies beneath.

How can you hope to manage different types of behaviour?

Let's be honest — you can't manage every possible behaviour problem.

Not on your own, anyway.

You are unlikely to see a vast range of complex behaviours all in one go. A child in your class may have significant needs that affect how he or she behaves, but you should receive support for this from your school's SENCO (special educational needs coordinator) or inclusion leader.

Within a mainstream classroom, it is more common to have to deal with what is affectionately known as 'low-level disruption'.

That term sounds incredibly...broad.

But you'll recognise it as children talking when they should be working, arguing in the line about who should be at the front, or drawing on a whiteboard instead of trying to work out the answer to the maths question.

Low-level disruption can take more energy to manage than more complex cases. Why? Because it occurs most frequently.

The child in the class who is always irritating others by poking them on the carpet or pushing them in the playground requires your more frequent attention. The children who display this kind of behaviour are the ones that need firm boundaries from the very first day, and you must provide these.

These children respond best to the three principles discussed in the previous chapter: respect, humour, and consistency.

What if I don't understand why a child is behaving in a certain way?

Children are complex creatures. As an NQT, you aren't expected to understand all the reasons for their behaviour. Even the most experienced teachers may find it difficult to fully unpick what could be at the heart of the problem.

As a teacher in your first year, you won't just have more experienced members of staff around you, but also your mentor. They can help you determine what may be causing persistently difficult behaviour.

It is always helpful if you come up with your own thoughts and ideas, rather than expecting your mentor to provide the solutions to your many questions and difficulties.

Can you talk to the teacher who had that child or class the previous year? This isn't always possible if that member of staff has left or you teach reception or nursery. However, if you can talk to the previous teacher, he or she may be able to give you some further tips to manage the class as a whole or the individual children who cause the most disruption to your lessons.

Asking for advice isn't a sign of weakness or inexperience. It is purely a sign that you want to manage the children or child in the best way possible. Senior staff would rather you were proactive in finding answers than expect solutions to come via a magic wand which will make these children disappear.

Mistakes

A common mistake is making a big deal about all low-level disruption. You will need to handle some situations quickly and, more importantly, without disrupting too much of the learning. This is why it is crucial to be able to think on your feet and adapt to the situation.

For your own energy levels, you will need to learn which battles to fight.

The strategies that appear later in this book will help you know what might work and when.

Action steps

1. Remember that all behaviour is communication. Ask yourself what the child is trying to tell you.

2. Use the Iceberg Model to determine why a child could be behaving in a certain way or why his or her behaviour might have changed.

3. Use the experience of staff and other professionals around you to help you unpick a child's behaviour and to think of strategies that might work for that individual pupil.

4. Remember that what worked for one difficult situation may not work for another. Try to be adaptable and think on your feet when a difficult situation presents itself. This comes with practise and, ultimately, confidence.

Read on, Macduff!

The next chapter looks further at you, the teacher. How can you instill a sense of self-belief in your practice? How can you create a 'presence' in the classroom? These skills will ensure that you can tackle any behaviour that presents itself.

CHAPTER 3

Self-Belief

A 2014 survey found that 42 per cent of UK teachers are leaving the profession after the end of their second year. A shocking statistic isn't it, but one that isn't going away. The blame seems to lie with the workload and pressure to meet targets.

Managing behaviour is just another part of the job that can be time-consuming and stressful. But it doesn't have to be, and this book aims to make it as pain-free as possible. You need to believe in your ability to manage a class of children and believe that your principles and style will ensure that you don't become one of the 42 per cent - and certainly not due to the stresses of managing your class.

What can you expect from effectively managing children's behaviour?

You know that Friday feeling?

You come in from your placement school, kick off your shoes, and sink into the armchair with a glass of your favourite tipple. You're exhausted and so grateful it's the weekend.

Time to face the truth. Your job is not going to get any less tiring in your NQT year.

Teaching is bloody exhausting. If you're not planning, you're marking; if you're not marking, you're assessing. Or photocopying. Or filling in targets. Or talking to parents. The list goes on...

Behaviour management is just another part of the job that you have to do. It is hard work, and you have to put in the time and the effort. But there is one great thing about it: behaviour management is difficult, tiring, and time-consuming for only a relatively short amount of time.

Why? Because once you've got your systems in place and have consistently stuck to them, behaviour management becomes easy. Your first year (and beyond) will be much easier if you get it right from the very first day. Heck, even the very first minute.

So, what can you expect from effectively managing children's behaviour? Here are just a few characteristics that spring to mind:

- An environment that is conducive to teaching and learning

- A trust that your class will behave appropriately wherever they are

- A sense of respect and teamwork within the classroom

- A teaching week that focuses on the most important thing, children's learning, and not managing low-level disruption

- Confidence in your ability to manage behaviour that will continue with you throughout your years of teaching

If you feel as though these characteristics sound too difficult to achieve, and you can't imagine ever feeling this way, I may have the answer for you: acting.

Why is it important to remember that teaching is a form of acting?

As you well know, to 'act' means to take on the role of a character. There are many times when a teacher has to 'act' when responding to a behaviour choice or situation. You will have to respond according to the school's behaviour policy, to ensure that there is consistency across the school.

Let's consider a school's approach to uniform.

At my school, we follow the principle of 'look smart, work smart.' This principle of a child's uniform looking smart extends to the three hundred or so children at my school.

Personally, I believe that looking smart makes you ready for learning and gives children a sense of pride in their appearance.

Some of you may have read my opinion and nodded sagely, agreeing with my every word. Others of you may have thought, 'Why on earth is she so bothered about uniform?' The fact is, if smart uniform is not at the heart of your behaviour principles, but the school policy adopts a 'look smart, work smart' approach, you're going to have to act your socks off to stick with the policy, i.e. reminding the children to tuck their shirts in when you're really not that bothered.

Now acting in the role of a teacher who is concerned about uniform is one thing. Acting like a confident teacher facing a class of new children is quite another.

There is only one word that can justify what is needed, and that is:

Presence.

We can also call this assertiveness. You need to have presence or assertiveness in the classroom or the children will eat you alive, quite possibly with your teaching assistant for dessert.

You may not feel like you have this magical thing called 'presence', and you may not naturally be able to produce it. But the good thing is, you can act like you have oodles of the stuff coming out of every pore.

How can you create presence?

Entrepreneur Malcolm Forbes (creator of Forbes Magazine) once said, 'Presence is more than just being there.'

Think back to your days at school. Were there teachers who just had a 'presence' in the classroom? When they walked in, everyone fell silent. You knew their footsteps in the corridor, since their walk sounded purposeful and measured. They never appeared flustered, were always punctual, and had that look that could silence the loudest child.

Now think of teachers who didn't have presence — the ones who came in with half their lunch down their shirt, books spilling out of their bag, a flustered look on their face. They had a quiet and unassuming tone of voice, and no one realised they had entered the room to start a lesson. Pupils showed them no respect, and you could tell the other staff didn't take them too seriously either.

Which of these teachers would you rather be?

Two key things will help you develop a presence or assertiveness in your classroom:

Body language. The way you hold yourself will tell the children that you mean business. Don't walk in with rounded shoulders, looking at the floor and avoiding eye contact. Do walk purposefully with your shoulders back and your head held high.

When talking to children, give them direct eye contact and listen with your whole body. That's right, your whole body. Turn to face them, have a look of genuine interest (even if it's the third time they have told you about their holiday), and give them the impression that you have time for them. If they feel you have time for them, they will have time for your strategies, your teaching, and your ideas.

Voice. Voice projection is absolutely crucial to your success with teaching, both in behaviour management and in delivering lessons. It is so important that you look after your voice and use it correctly. In order to have a voice that matches the body language described above, follow these tips carefully:

- Make sure you speak from the base of your stomach, not from your throat. Push your voice out from there.

- Have a water bottle in your classroom that you sip from frequently — even when you don't feel particularly thirsty. Doing so will stop your throat from getting dry and damaged and will protect your vocal cords.

- No teacher should rely on shouting as a behaviour management strategy. However, there may be times when you need to raise your voice to get the class's attention, like when outside for PE. Shout from your belly; otherwise, if you shout from just your throat, your voice will sound strained.

- When you use the 'shoulders back' technique mentioned above, your voice will naturally project louder than if you stand with rounded shoulders. Ladies, stick out your assets…

A brilliant book about using your voice is *Set Your Voice Free* by Roger Love - you can get a copy on Amazon. I recommend you read it if you want further support.

What if the children see through your acting?

I can see why this question would be asked, but my natural response would be: do you think that children in primary schools are seriously going to consider whether or not you're acting the character of 'teacher who manages behaviour well'?

Some of the older children can sense nerves, but when it's the first day, they are nervous too. The first day is often the most worrying for children, as it normally means new teacher, new classroom, and sometimes, new peers. How you're feeling and how nervous you are won't even cross their minds.

The more you act your role (if that is what you feel you need to do), the more natural it will become. Practise the body language and, if you can bear it, stand in front of a mirror and look at yourself. Hunch your shoulders and recoil into yourself (which may well represent exactly how you feel about managing behaviour). Then stand upright, shoulders back, head high, and see the difference. You may feel like the world's most daft teacher, but it's worth it. No one will know if you reach for that hairbrush and belt out a chart-topping ballad either, so do whatever is necessary to get used to a confident stance.

The more you see yourself with positive, confident body language, the more likely you are to walk in on that very first day with your head held high.

Looking after your emotional well-being

Managing the behaviour of your class can be stressful and tiring, particularly as an NQT. You may feel an immense amount of pressure to get it right and your frustrations might come out in the ways that you respond to the children. We can all act disappointed when a child makes a poor behaviour choice, but sometimes you might feel genuinely frustrated by it, particularly when you have spent time helping a pupil find solutions to managing their emotions effectively.

If you find yourself snapping at the children and losing patience with them on a regular basis, then I would advise you to talk to someone you trust about it. Teaching children is hard work, and even the best teachers can let it get on top of them. Be a reflective teacher and try to be aware of whether negative emotions are getting on top of you frequently. It isn't good for your health, and it isn't good for your class.

And the award goes to…

On a daily basis, I often have to turn into my alter ego, affectionately called Bad Cop. Bad Cop is frequently called in an emergency, often when a teacher feels that the situation is out of control, such as when a physical fight erupts in the playground.

Bad Cop swoops in to deal with the situation. For the younger children, Bad Cop just has to give them a warning look and sometimes have her hands on her hips. She talks in a very low tone and sounds as though she expects answers. When Bad Cop approaches, the younger children know it's serious. She means business.

The older children know that Bad Cop is important in the school and not just 'assembly lady' as the youngest children often call her. A warning look can sometimes do the job with the less frequent offenders, but there are times when Bad Cop will take away their playtime or will phone their parents. The older children also know that she means business, and only the brave argue back.

But Bad Cop is just a character. I don't genuinely feel cross about the fact that X threw Y's lunch on the floor or that A told B his mum was fat. Quite often I am disappointed, but never am I genuinely angry. Never do I raise my voice or get into children's personal space, and I always let the children know that I will hear their side of the story.

Unfortunately, some members of staff rely on Bad Cop so much and require her to attend so many emergencies that her other job (Good Cop, deputy head, SENCO, teacher) goes out the window. Be the teacher who manages behaviour effectively, who has read this book and has those strategies in place, so that you rarely call on Bad Cop, and when you do, it is for something truly serious.

Mistakes

I have suggested you 'act' in your role of 'teacher who manages behaviour well' in a bid for you to start to manage behaviour naturally. I stand by this and think it is important.

However, what is also important is to realise that you are acting. Having high expectations of behaviour is, as you will see, crucial to behaviour management working in the classroom. But if you begin to find that you are consistently responding negatively towards the children and their choices in behaviour, it is time to take a step back.

Children are human beings, after all, and they learn from the mistakes they make. Hopefully these mistakes guide them to understand how to act as adults. Don't pick up on every little thing they do; the children will feel as though they are walking on eggshells. Let mistakes happen and allow children to learn from them.

The way you manage behaviour can affect your health and well-being. If you tackle every small thing, you will exhaust yourself, and that is not sustainable. The joy will go out of teaching, and you'll forget why you joined the profession. Have high expectations, yes, but don't feel as though you are bound to them every second of every day. As well as accepting that the children will make mistakes, you need to accept that you will make them too. Learn from them and allow them to help you develop into a truly effective practitioner.

Action steps

1. Remember that the art of acting can help you, especially if you don't feel that you naturally 'get' behaviour management.

2. Practise body language and presence. Stand in front of the mirror, have purpose in each stride, and you will soon develop a natural way of 'being' in the classroom.

3. If you feel yourself getting genuinely frustrated with the children much of the time, take a step back and seek advice. What are the triggers that make you feel this way? Is anything going on for you personally that could be affecting how you deal with behaviour?

4. Allow children to make mistakes, and help them use their mistakes as a learning opportunity. Help them to develop the skills they need to be global citizens in today's world.

5. When you start your new job, ask your mentor whether there are any outstanding behaviour management practitioners in the school. If so, arrange to observe them. Reading about different strategies is one thing; seeing them in action is quite another.

Read on, Macduff!

The following chapter outlines my SIMPLE approach to behaviour management, which I designed to help you develop your own unique style when managing your class. It also gives examples of how you can use it best within your classroom.

CHAPTER 4

The SIMPLE Approach to Behaviour Management – Part 1

To help you develop a behaviour management system that is quick to implement, I have devised an approach that is as easy as ABC. I have written it to ensure you have an approach that works and will build your confidence. It is called the SIMPLE approach to behaviour management, and you can use it from the very first day. SIMPLE stands for:

S — Systems

I — Implementation of class rules

M — Management

P — Pace

L — Language

E — Expectations

I have broken each one of these down for you to read through, to get a better understanding of how you can use this approach in your classroom. This chapter is devoted entirely to the importance of systems. Get that pen ready; this is where the planning really starts.

S — Systems

Set up systems from the very first day, as children respond well to them. This is crucial to your behaviour management becoming second nature to you and the class, but it takes some planning. You need to think of the systems that are going to work for you and that are simple to set up and maintain.

Reward system. Design your reward system around a team approach. An example of this could be: each table is a team and can think of their own team name. Each team has a captain and vice-captain that change each week. The job of the captain is to facilitate how the members of the team work. They must work together effectively to ensure that the table is tidy, they are ready to learn, and they follow the class rules. The teams could compete to win marbles to put in their team jar. The team with the most marbles at the end of the week can be awarded 'table of the week' stickers. A tally chart is just as effective and doesn't need to be fancy. A Year 6 colleague of mine uses an online resource called 'Class Dojo.' This not only keeps 'dojo points' for class behaviour, it also allows parents to see how well their child is behaving in the classroom and they are encouraged to access this from home. Find it at www.classdojo.com.

Seating plan. How are you going to seat the children? Are you going to let them sit with their friends on the first day so you can work out who works well together and who doesn't? Or are you going to create a seating plan based on the information given to you by the previous teacher?

I recommend a seating plan to ensure effective learning takes place. Organise tables so that no one will have their back to you or the board. Base the seating plan on your knowledge of the children or notes from the previous teacher. Write names on Post-it notes to stick on tables so that children know where to sit on the first day. Let them know that they will stay in these seats for the first week. Then move them based on your observations and understanding of the individual children. They don't have to stay in these seats all year; you can even swap them each half term to give children opportunities to work with a range of peers.

Random name generator. This tool is a generator that

randomly picks a child's name and flashes it onto the interactive whiteboard or computer screen. That child will then answer your question or share their ideas with the class. As well as a good Assessment for Learning (AfL) strategy, this is a good tool to use to ensure that the class are always focused in on what you are doing, as they never know if their name will be chosen. There are lots of random name generators online – simply type the phrase into your search engine to find one. Personally, I have used the one at www.superteachertools.com.

Class responsibilities. These could include register monitors, homework monitors and book monitors. Make sure that you explain to the children what these roles entail so that they can do the jobs effectively. Also make sure that every child gets a turn at something throughout the year – children are very aware of this element of fairness, so make sure you keep a list of who has done what as the year goes on.

Class rules. Think about what you want these rules to be. You don't want to have too many, otherwise it will be difficult to remember them all. I recommend you have approximately six – there will be school rules for the children to be aware of too, so you don't want to overload them. The children should be actively involved in creating the rules (see Chapter 6) but you should guide them to the principles you think the class must have.

Carpet spaces. These are particularly useful for younger children as you can place pupils where you need them to be on the carpet. If there are children who find it hard to concentrate, have them near the front so that you can manage their behaviour easily. It can also be a good strategy to ensure mixed ability learning.

Learning pupils' names. Provide sticky labels with children's names and ask them to wear these on the first day. Learn everyone's name by the end of the day and then throw the labels away. You *must* know all names by the end of day one.

Morning routine. What are you expecting from your class when they first arrive in the morning? Have something for them to do rather than letting them mill around until it is time for you to do the register. This activity, of course, will depend on their age. But with training, you can introduce a variety of activities that ensure children are ready to learn at nine o'clock. These could be responding to marking, reading, or answering a 'daily challenge' or a question that will extend their higher order thinking.

Lining up for moving around the school. When children line up for lunch or assembly, or to come back into the classroom, you need to tell them what your expectations are. Some teachers develop a specific line order, deliberately putting (or not putting) certain children together, to ensure that they move around the school silently. Other teachers line pupils up in register order. With the older children, it can be fun to mix this up a bit — for example, sometimes lining them up by first name and sometimes by surname. It gets their brains working and keeps the idea from becoming tedious. The idea of 'boy, girl, boy, girl' can work effectively, provided you work in a mixed school, of course! A quiet line when returning to the classroom will ensure a calm start to each lesson, with all children ready to learn.

Stopping the class. There is a range of methods for this, from cowbells to counting down from five to zero. Clapping rhythms, songs, and tambourines can also be used effectively. Whatever your method is for stopping the class, keep it consistent and let the children know what to do when they hear that cue. Practise it explicitly on the first day so that you can make sure it is done as well as you expect. Make sure that all of the children follow the rules for stopping. Don't let one person get away with not doing it properly, as this can spread. Ensure that other adults in the room use the same strategy as you to ensure consistency.

Sanctions. I deliberately put the reward system at the top of this list because I think your systems need to be based on rewards primarily. However, with a reward system must come a sanction system. Follow the school's behaviour policy on this one, because you want to make sure that the children understand this from a whole school perspective: whichever class they are in, the same system for behaviour applies to everyone. But there are some sanctions that can be put into place in your own room that match your principles and style. One example is the Three Strikes Rule.

The Three Strikes Rule

Using the Three Strikes Rule in your class could serve you well, as it is simple for the children to understand and for you to follow. Each of the three strikes is more serious than the previous one. This enables you to build up to a sanction without seeming as though you have just leapt straight into the most serious one. Again, you are aiming for consistency and fairness.

STRIKE 1: The Look. A warning look is, by far and away, one of the most effective strategies in a classroom. Often it is all that is needed, and you won't need to go on to Strike 2 or 3. The trick behind The Look is to make it deliberate. You might hold eye contact with that child for just a second or two longer than feels comfortable. You might pause what you are saying, just briefly, to emphasise the point that the child you are looking at is interrupting the lesson. The Look can sound quite ominous, but actually it isn't. It is a way of managing a situation without using your voice — too much of that, and the children will switch off.

STRIKE 2: The Warning. A verbal warning is the next strike. It can often be accompanied by another instance of The Look. The tone of your voice should be low and measured. If you start squeaking or rushing your words, you will appear out of control.

Start your warning with the words, "I'm sorry, children, but X is interrupting our lesson, and I'm going to have to stop what we're doing." Then address the child directly and say something like, "Is there a problem?" What happens next depends on the response to this question.

If there is a problem, don't attempt to solve it there and then (unless it is a simple solution, like moving the child away from someone nearby who is being annoying). Assure the child that the two of you will speak about the problem at the end of the lesson, but not now, as there is learning to do. Make sure you do follow up so that the child feels valued and listened to.

More likely, the response to 'Is there a problem?' will be a shake of the head. In that case, request that the child apologise to the class for the interruption, and then wait. Thank the child for the apology and finish with, "If you continue to interrupt, you will need to speak to me at break" (or lunchtime). The warning is there — it is up to the child to make the right behaviour choices after that.

STRIKE 3: The Choice. This is the easiest way to deal with persistent low-level disruption: put the behaviour back on the child and make it his or her responsibility. You will give the child two choices for how to behave.

For example, suppose Fred is persistently talking or distracting others at the table. Crouch down next to him and speak quietly but firmly. Don't humiliate a child in front of the class. We're here to encourage the right behaviour, not humiliate and embarrass children for the wrong behaviour.

The conversation with Fred could sound something like this: "Now, I have already warned you about your behaviour. I am going to give you two choices, and I encourage you to choose the right one. The first choice is that you stop distracting those people around you and get on with the work I have asked you to do. The second choice is that you carry on distracting them, but then I will tell you to move to another place. Which choice is it?" Other possibilities for the second choice might be that the child must move to another classroom or continue working during break or lunchtime.

Now, to be honest, I have never had a child say, "Option 2, please, Miss. I am going to be a distraction to everyone." Choosing that option would be fairly bold! Fred will most likely select option 1.

Ask him to repeat the chosen option back to you so that he is completely aware of what you are expecting. Give him the chance to carry out that option. However, if he persists with a poor choice of behaviour, despite the word you have had with him, it is time to do the most important thing in behaviour management: FOLLOW THROUGH WITH WHAT YOU HAVE SAID. Now I know I am shouting, but I want you to remember this and never, ever allow yourself to back down.

If you have said Fred will work in another classroom, take him there with his work and leave him to get on with it. If you have said he will need to come back at lunchtime to complete the work he has missed, ensure he comes back at lunch. If you don't follow through with the second choice he is offered, he won't take you seriously and will know that he can get away with that behaviour on another occasion – as will the other children.

I will say it once more, just to clarify: FOLLOW THROUGH WITH WHAT YOU HAVE SAID. Got it? Good. I will put my megaphone away now…

You can use the term 'Three Strikes Rule' with the class so that they know this is the sanction system. Explain it clearly and calmly on the first day. When you give verbal warnings, tell children that this is Strike 2, so that they know where they are in your class behaviour system.

With certain Year 6 classes, you could add the tag line, 'Three strikes and you're out.' This doesn't mean that they sit outside the classroom door, staring into space. It means they are moved to another learning environment to continue their work. If that is the deputy head's office, then so be it. But they won't be able to continue their work in your classroom. Be tough on that, and your pupils will soon get the message.

Read on, Macduff!

The next chapter looks at the other aspects of the SIMPLE approach to ensure that you have a good understanding of how best to implement it. This includes:

I — Implementation of class rules

M — Management

P — Pace

L — Language

E — Expectations

CHAPTER 5

The SIMPLE Approach to Behaviour Management – Part 2

I — Implementation of class rules

As explained previously, children need boundaries in order to thrive. As they grow older, boundaries will be put into place in all walks of life, and they will need to respond appropriately. You can teach them this skill by implementing class rules.

On the first day with your new class, create some class rules that you can all stick to. Here are the key things to remember when setting up rules for your classroom:

- Create the rules together so that the children have ownership.

- Emphasise that the rules must be followed by everyone in the class — adults too!

- Phrase the rules positively, such as 'We take turns to speak in the class' rather than 'Don't call out.'

- Ensure that mutual respect is a class rule. Explain that concept to all year groups so that everyone is clear about what it means.

- Have all members of the class — including adults — sign the rules to show their agreement to stick to them.

- Display the rules in a prominent place. Refer to them often so that children can see you using them to ensure consistency and fairness.

Rules for adults

Some teachers have two sets of rules or expectations: what the teacher expects from the children and what the children expect from the teacher. This is quite a nice strategy to use with older children. If you make a mistake, you can refer back to the expectations the class set for you and admit that maybe you didn't quite stick to that one. Admitting a mistake takes bravery, but it demonstrates the mutual respect and accountability that needs to be embedded.

Expectations that have been set for me as a teacher include:

• Be fair.

• Mark our work so that we can receive regular feedback.

• Make our lessons fun and exciting.

• Help us when we are stuck.

• Have a sense of humour.

• Give us rewards when we deserve them.

These expectations were from a Year 6 class, and you can see that they came up with some great ideas. Younger children can come up with similar ideas but may need help phrasing them carefully.

M — Management

We've addressed some of this in the systems section in the previous chapter, but managing low-level disruption deserves its own section. Fail to manage it, and you're asking for a difficult start to your teaching career.

Ofsted are keen to tackle this type of disruption. In 2014 they published a report about it called 'Below the Radar: low-level disruption in the country's classrooms'. If inspectors from Ofsted are observing one of your lessons, they will expect to see you deal with any disruption in an effective and confident way.

So, what is 'low-level disruption'? Here are some clear examples that you may experience:

Talking whilst the teacher is talking. This behaviour is so common that I am sure you have witnessed it. Under no circumstances should you let this happen. It is a little bit like a germ — once one person comes down with the 'talking bug', it will quickly spread around the classroom. Managing this behaviour comes back to high expectations, and your response should be absolutely non-negotiable. Do not address the class or give out instructions or take the register if children are talking. Do not let children feed back their ideas or answers if other people are talking. Create a listening culture: when someone is speaking, we listen to them with our whole body.

Not following a system that has been taught. If you have explained and practised a particular system, such as walking up the stairs silently after break time, you should expect it to happen this way every single time. If the children start to think they can chat during this process, and you don't address it, they will continue to do it. Remind them of your expectations, If they continue to go against the class rules, get them to repeat the action in the way you want it to be done, such as going back downstairs and coming up again silently. You could add the possibility of practising this in 'their time' — that is, break time — and 'not in my time.'

P — Pace

Have you ever sat through something that made you want to curl into a small ball and pretend you were on a sunny beach somewhere? Maybe it was a long, boring film or something you were taken to see that really wasn't your thing at all. You looked at your watch and hoped that it would all be over soon. You fidgeted in your seat, you began to think about the list of things you needed to get done that week, or, if you're anything like my father, you simply fell asleep.

When I have sat in a meeting for a few hours, I get restless and fidgety. I don't listen to what is being said, and I keep looking at the clock on the wall. Sometimes I might doodle in my notebook or draw pretty patterns all over the agenda. Whatever I'm doing, I am not giving my full attention to the meeting.

Now put yourself in the shoes of children in your class who have to sit in your lessons for five hours a day, every day, whether they enjoy the subject or not. If the lessons move at a slow pace, the likelihood of the children becoming disruptive grows quite considerably. Do you blame them?

There are two definitive ways to tell whether your pace has slowed:

The Velcro Test. As soon as you hear Velcro being pulled on a pair of shoes, you know you have lost the attention of at least one child in the class. That sound should give you the cue to either wrap things up or give the children a 'brain break'. That might mean directing pupils to discuss the lesson with a talk partner or, if appropriate, sending them to get on with the work at their tables. Admittedly, the Velcro Test tends to work better in Key Stage 1, before children learn to tie laces!

Movement of key children. You know who I mean: the children in the class who have the shortest attention spans. We're not talking only about the children with special educational needs, but any who need support for focusing. As soon as rolling, lounging, or low-level chatting starts while you are presenting your lesson, you need to think on your feet. Have you done enough talking to enable children to access the independent activity? Some schools have guidance about lesson structure and create a rule that children are not kept on the carpet for more than ten minutes.

Here are some ways to keep your lessons moving:

- Give children time limits to complete tasks – use a timer to give them a visual reminder of how much time is left.

- Set clear time expectations: "In one minute we are going to line up at the door silently."

- Ensure that you follow the 80:20 rule: You want the children to be doing the majority of the talking, with you just guiding the learning and discussion with well-planned questions.

Warning! Understanding pace takes practise. If lessons are presented too fast, children will become confused. If they are too slow, children lose interest and don't understand what to do when the time comes for independent work. Low-level disruption also thrives if the pace is too slow. Don't be afraid to let your lesson take a different route when responding to children's understanding. Doing so can help with the pace problem. Respond to the needs of the class on any given day, and your pace should develop effectively.

L — Language

Now I am sure some of you read this heading and thought, 'I know not to swear at the children; calling them little b*stards will make me lose my job.' But that isn't what I mean, although I strongly advise you to keep it clean!

What I mean here is relatively simple in theory but quite difficult in practice: don't use too much language when dealing with behaviour. This advice works well not only for children with autism, but all children.

Be crystal clear about your expectations. Don't use fancy words in your class rules. Don't use long sentences when explaining why you're disappointed with a child. The child will switch off, and you'll vow to go home and stay silent for the evening, as you'll be sick of the sound of your own voice. That is why The Look can work so well — it saves so much talking.

The 80:20 rule works well here too. In this case, it states that 80 per cent of effective behaviour management comes from using 20 per cent of the language available to you.

Try not to get dragged into a discussion with a child whose behaviour you are trying to manage. The child will only think you're open to negotiation, which YOU ARE NOT (oops, that megaphone is back). If a child tries to argue with me, I simply raise an eyebrow with a look of pure shock on my face. (To be fair, I am only able to raise only one eyebrow, but I don't want you to think that raising two is any less effective.) The look of surprise on my face will normally be enough to stop the child from continuing to argue. If not, I can say, "I'm sorry, are you arguing with me?" That will stop most children in their tracks.

E — Expectations

You may have noticed that I use the term 'expectations' a lot, and with good reason. You, too, need to use it when talking to children. This word has to become a key part of your vocabulary, particularly with the word 'high' inserted before it. Use phrases like, "What I am expecting from you is..." or "You know that I expect you to..." Keep this word in your vocabulary, and it will soon become part of theirs.

If you let your high expectations slip, all that hard work that you put in at the beginning of the year will be undone. Your expectations need to be as high on the last day of the year as they are on the first. The great thing is that the children will know what these expectations are and will rise to meet them, if you are consistent and persistent.

What if the children start to ignore the SIMPLE approach?

All classes will test the boundaries of the SIMPLE plan, because children want to see how far they can go. Testing these boundaries is natural; we even do it as adults when we start a new job or a new hobby. Luckily, by the time we have reached adulthood, most of us are able to understand when it is or isn't acceptable to test boundaries. Some children are aware of this too, but others will see how far they can push you.

Be prepared and stick to your principles. If you expect children to test you and plan how you might react, you will be better prepared when the inevitable happens. Hopefully, the testing of boundaries will come from low-level disruption rather than a full-blown incident.

Low-level disruption can be when your 'Three Strikes Rule' comes into play. Be clear, consistent, and clarify your expectations of behaviour. Remind children of the rules that you generated together; point to them on your display if you have to. Use the rules to explain why you are giving them a warning or asking them to move rooms. They signed the contract; they abide by the rules. It is as simple as that. Do not budge from the rules you have put in place, and do not move away from your principles that you have worked so hard to develop. Be stubborn!

Remind yourself of this principle: 'My classroom, my rules.' You wouldn't let someone into your home to shout at you, write on the walls, or mock your prize possessions. Why would you allow someone be disrespectful in your classroom? See this room as an extension of your home — to be fair, you spend more time there than you do at home, so this shouldn't be difficult! I am not suggesting you share the 'My classroom, my rules' phrase with your pupils, but you could adapt it to 'This is *our* classroom and these are *our* rules.'

Should inappropriate behaviour persist, you may need a senior teacher or leader to remind children of the school rules. We will come to that in chapter 10.

Creating and managing 'buzz'

Your aim is to engage the children in well-planned, motivating lessons that result in progression for all pupils. To accomplish this goal, you need to generate some excitement around learning, or what my head teacher calls 'buzz'. But to create 'buzz', you need to be brave, you need to be bold, and you need behaviour management. Without it, 'buzz' soon becomes chaos, and no learning takes place whatsoever.

The SIMPLE approach ensures that when you generate a learning buzz, you know you can bring your class back from real excitement to produce effective learning. The key is being consistent and keeping to your principles and expectations whenever the children are engaged in a lively and exciting activity.

Earlier I mentioned the importance of having a system in place for stopping the class. This becomes even more important in activities that generate a lot of movement, discussion, and excitement, such as PE. Take your system with you wherever you go, so the children know what is expected of them in any environment; class trips, PE lessons or when a visitor to the school generates 'buzz'. Bear in mind that if you use a tambourine to stop activity, it has to go everywhere with you, which can prove difficult at times – you can have a back-up strategy in place for PE (e.g. counting back from 10) and this can then be transferred to other environments too.

Mistakes

One of the biggest mistakes teachers can make with their behaviour plan is becoming complacent — thinking that their plan is firmly embedded after only a few weeks. It isn't. You can normally begin to relax a little in the spring term, but definitely not before then. By the time the spring term arrives, children will know your boundaries and how far they can go before warnings come into play. Some classes pick this up quicker and some take longer, but they will all get there in the end.

Think of this as the Cellophane Effect — stick to your principles the way cellophane sticks to your fingers when you unwrap something new. It doesn't come off no matter how hard you shake. Don't make the mistake of thinking that your pupils are ready for you to relax; it's a long time until July, and it will feel even longer if you've lost them due to poor or inconsistent behaviour management.

Action steps

1. Use the SIMPLE approach to set up behaviour management in your class.

2. Set up your systems and stick to them — be consistent and persistent.

3. Remember the Cellophane Effect — stick to your principles.

4. Don't make the mistake of becoming relaxed too soon. The first term should be the hardest, but you will reap the rewards for the next two terms, and your class will become better able to work within that 'learning buzz'.

Read on, Macduff!

Now that you have learnt about the SIMPLE approach to behaviour management in the classroom, it is time to put it all to the test and tackle day one with your new class. The next chapter will help you to find your behaviour management style from the very first day.

CHAPTER 6

The First Day

First day nerves — they're a real treat, aren't they?

Sleepless nights beforehand, dreams about the class ignoring your every word, an inability to eat breakfast… the list goes on.

I have been teaching for ten years, my husband for even longer, and we both still get like this on 31st August. Why? Because we want the first day to go right. We want the children to respond to us, to learn from us, and to look forward to the year ahead.

Here is a transcript from a note I received from a Year 6 child on the last day of the summer term, just before she left to go to secondary school. It meant so much to me that I have kept it after all these years:

Mrs Caswell,

Thank you for being a lovely teacher and for helping me so much this year. I have really enjoyed getting to know you; you are a fabulous person.

On the first day when you said, "tuck your shirt in" to me, I thought "oh no" this is going to be a rough year, but how wrong was I? You have been so wonderful, kind, caring and funny! I will miss you!

Lots of love, Lauren

Looks like I wasn't the only one who was nervous, right?

That's the key thing to remember. You may have been having bad dreams, trips to the toilet, a sudden urge to be violently sick, but what about the children? They are preparing for a new teacher, one that they haven't seen a lot of before and don't know much about. Will you be scary? Strict? Kind? Will you remember their names? Most of all, will they like you and will you like them?

It all comes down to that very first day.

Get that right, and the rest of the week, term, and year will be far easier.

What to expect on the first day

I am going to be brutally honest.

The first day will be like a dream.

Stop rubbing your eyes — you read that right. It won't be like the stomach-churning, palpitation-inducing dream I mentioned at the very start of this book. The first day gives you a sense of security; filling your head with the thought that this class is like no other you have met or taught before.

Let me be clear: it is a *false* sense of security.

On the first day, the children will want to impress you. Even the grumpiest Year 6 pupil will give it a whirl. Children need and want to be liked (as do we), and they will spend that first day making you think that all the notes you wrote during the handover with their previous teacher must be about the wrong class. No rubbers are being thrown and no one is calling out. Surely she must have been talking about a different class?

Quite possibly, but the other option is that you are currently in what I affectionately call the Honeymoon Period.

The Honeymoon Period is like the first few months of a new relationship. Nothing the other person does gets on your nerves; you listen to one another, you make every effort to look your best, and you try really hard to make the other person feel special.

This is exactly what the first day with your new class is like. If I could put fairy dust and twinkly lights on this page, I would. Maybe even a bit of harp music playing in the background…

Sounds magical, doesn't it? Enjoy it.

Why the first day is actually the easiest day of all

Now I may have painted a rather rosy picture of the first day, but actually you must use the Honeymoon Period as your ticket to the start of a fantastic year with your class.

This is the day to put all your behaviour plans into place.

Actually, the first minute is the time to start putting your behaviour plans into place.

Take heed of the following advice: 'Start as you mean to go on.'

Laying down the ground rules — the absolute rigidity of your high expectations — from the very first few minutes will stand you in good stead for continuing this way for the rest of the year.

An example is how you expect children to come in when they arrive in the morning. Perhaps you expect them to do an activity that you have left them to do, be it responding to marking, answering a challenge question, or simply reading their books. Put this into practice from the first day. Stand at the door and greet the pupils as they come in. Direct them to their peg or locker and then ask them to find the seat with their name on a sticky note. Let them know that the instructions for what they need to do are on the board and they need to complete the activity whilst waiting for everyone to arrive.

Now this may sound regimented, but it lets your pupils know that each morning, this will be how things are done in your classroom. When you have done the register that very first morning, explain your expectation to them.

You may have heard the phrase, 'Don't smile till Christmas.' I don't subscribe to it fully, but I certainly don't let pupils see my more humorous side until the end of the autumn term. That very first morning, I will, of course, smile at them when they come in, but I keep everything quite business-like so they know that I am pleased to see them, but that my expectations are high.

If you teach Key Stage 1, you might think that what I have described above isn't possible.

Well, I hate to break it to you, but it is. You will need to work harder to get the children into a morning routine, but it can work, and they will be able to do it independently. They just need training.

How to plan for the first day

You will no doubt prepare for the first day with some planning of the academic kind. I want you to think about how you might make a plan of the behavioural kind, e.g. How will you fit in time on that first day to set up the behaviour principles that you expect your class to adhere to? Where are you going to display these rules so that they can be referred to? Plan a circle time session for that first day, to ensure you devote some quality time to creating these rules with the children.

The importance of planning the first day is to ensure that you feel more prepared and that you are clear about your strategies for combating low-level disruption. Planning will make you feel more in control of the group, and the children will respond to someone setting those clear boundaries right from the start.

Feeling prepared

Give yourself enough time to prepare for your first day. As well as planning displays and activities, really sit down and think through what you want the behaviour of your class to look like. Using your knowledge of the SIMPLE approach, what do you want that class to look like by October half-term or Christmas?

If you can, share your ideas with another teacher and ask for their opinions. You will feel more confident having talked it all through, and your plans should then become clearer in your head. If possible, meet your mentor before the summer break and ask for advice. If you are able to get into your new school in the summer term, prior to your starting, ask to watch a more experienced teacher and pick up any behaviour tips that you think you could try.

Don't confuse first-day nerves with not being prepared. You may not feel prepared, and you may wish that you had spent more time on planning. But when you are thrown in with your class, you will be surprised how much your planning pays off, even if you did only a small amount.

The better prepared you are, the more in control you will feel, and that will mean the class feels in control too. Don't rush the planning stage. Think through it and do what you feel comfortable with. This should help you feel prepared and confident for that first day. I can't promise you won't have strange dreams, though, or feel the need to pace up and down nervously, waiting for the children to arrive. I would love to say that stops with experience, but...

As you become more experienced, your behaviour principles and expectations will be so embedded that you won't need this level of planning, but for now, get some ideas written down.

Mistakes

A common mistake you can make is not being prepared to take advantage of the good will of the children on the first day. They will try to impress you on that first day, and you need to use that to your advantage. Ensure you use as many opportunities as possible to praise the good behaviour choices that children have made; this will show them that you recognise the positive things that they do.

Bear in mind that the children are using day one to test you. The first thing they will talk about when they go into the playground at break time is their opinion of you. The first thing their parents will ask them on the way home is what they think of you.

You want them to report back a very positive experience. You are aiming to be firm but fair. They need to learn the expectations and boundaries, and they need to learn them quickly.

So be prepared. Make sure you have all your systems in place before day one and stick to them. Don't vary them either — keep them simple, and the children will respond. You don't want to look flustered, unprepared, and unsure. They will sense that and use it to their advantage, testing the boundaries far sooner than you are expecting them to.

I know I have made your pupils sound like a pack of hungry dogs, but in a way they are, and you are the leader of the pack. You need to face up to this, or your first year will be more stressful than it needs to be.

Action steps

1. Decide on your key behaviour principles. What do you want your class's behaviour to be like at the end of the first week? At the end of the first term?

2. Plan your routines and systems. For example, what beginning-of-day routine will you establish? What reward system will you use? Plan them and stick to them.

3. Plan a circle time session based on creating behaviour rules for the classroom. The more ownership the children have over the rules, the more likely they will stick to them. Display the rules as a reminder.

4. Talk through your plan with someone, such as your mentor. Does it sound manageable? Find out whether you need further advice on any children in your new class, such as those who have special educational needs or disabilities related to behaviour. If possible, observe more experienced staff to learn behaviour management tips.

Read on, Macduff!

Earlier on, I described the Honeymoon Period. The next chapter tackles what to do when this phase is over and how you can ride out the storm with ease.

CHAPTER 7

Maintaining Good Behaviour

The Honeymoon Period is like a dream.

One of those dreams when you wake up and you have to think long and hard about whether it was a dream or it actually happened.

Think of skipping through fields of tall grass in the middle of summer, picnic in hand and the day to yourself.

Everything you do, say, or request is met with a level of compliance from the children in your class. They smile, you smile...occasionally. Everything is right with the world.

How long the Honeymoon Period lasts is dependent on your class. Sometimes it is a few days or a week. Sometimes it is longer, if you're lucky.

Then one day, just like when the honeymoon ends for newly-weds, the first crack begins to show. Having the first row with your partner makes you come back to reality with a bump. And the first time your pupils tests the boundaries or rules you have established together can bring you back to Planet Teaching with just as hard a bump.

What to expect once the honeymoon is over

It is difficult to predict the first thing the class will do to test the boundaries you have so carefully put into place. Some signals might be:

• Not lining up quietly outside the door.

- Calling out during the teaching input.

- Not settling down to a task quickly.

- Coming in noisily in the morning and not doing the task you have left them to do.

The children who are going to be more difficult to manage might show these signals earlier, as they find boundaries harder to stick to. You will find yourself giving more constant reminders about your expectations — to some children more than others. You may even notice yourself feeling more exhausted at the end of a day because of how much effort you're putting into keeping your boundaries and expectations firm.

The key to overcoming these challenges is...KEEP GOING. Don't give up. Don't stop pushing forward with your principles and expectations. Don't let the children get away with ignoring one of the key classroom rules or principles — not even once.

Why it is important to be consistent and stick to your plan

I cannot stress highly enough the importance of consistency. Think back to the first chapter. What were the three key principles to effective classroom management?

- Respect

- Consistency

- Humour

Don't let these three principles out of your sight. They will keep you going through the tougher times. Keep them at the forefront of your behaviour management. Write them somewhere prominent. Tattoo them on your forehead if you must, but ignore them at your peril.

Consistency needs to be at the heart of behaviour management. Children need to know that if X happens, Y is the result. If they come in noisily, they will be asked to go back outside and come in appropriately.

Don't let them come in making a racket one day and then demand silence on the next. Inconsistency confuses children. It makes them feel uncertain, as they're never sure what the expectations are when they come into the classroom. It also makes you an ineffective teacher.

I once had a teacher who was inconsistent — not with managing my behaviour, but with how he would approach each lesson. One morning he would be all smiles, full of jokes, and approachable. The next morning, stony-faced and snappy. You never knew which style would greet you, and this was unsettling. You don't want your class to feel like that.

Let your children feel confident that they are going to get the same you, regardless of the day of the week, the weather outside or your personal problems. We all have days when things are not going right or we feel poorly, but it isn't the children's fault. If you're not well enough to be there, you shouldn't be there at all. Sounds harsh, but if you're unwell, you're not going to be performing at your best. Keeping the level of consistency up is harder when you have a stinking headache or you're full of cold. Don't be a martyr — look after yourself, and the rest will follow.

Being consistent from the beginning makes your job so much easier in the long term.

By Christmas (at the latest), you will have pupils who are not only easy to manage, but are able to do their best and most powerful learning. You are not wasting time or energy on trying to cope with low-level disruption. You are able to use your time to plan motivating and engaging lessons, whilst ensuring the children make the progress they need to each day.

How to manage when children come out of the Honeymoon Period

Your class will come out of the Honeymoon Period whether you like it or not, so you need to be ready.

Children want to feel safe, and they want someone to be in control. They are looking at you to provide this security. That is not to say they won't test the hell out of your boundaries.

But how do you get the children to stick to these boundaries? Simple. You train them.

Children are not born with an understanding of boundaries. They test them from the day they are born, so believe me, they will test you to see what your boundaries are. Be ready for that, and be ready to train them to know where your line is and what will happen if they cross it. Don't let the line get fuzzy; don't let the boundaries get blurred. If you stick to this strategy and a training regime, you will have a class ready and willing to learn.

Action steps

1. Be aware that the Honeymoon Period will end. Learn to recognise the signals that children are testing your boundaries.

2. Be consistent, both in how you manage behaviour and how you present yourself to children – keep to your SIMPLE approach.

3. Train children to know where your boundaries are and what happens if they cross them.

Read on, Macduff!

No behaviour management plan can take place effectively without the support of parents. The next chapter will focus on how to get great communication with parents, how to encourage them to support your principles at home, and what to do if a parent complains about a decision you have made.

CHAPTER 8

Working with Parents

Parents and behaviour management. What can I say? When it works well, it works brilliantly; when it doesn't, it can be a disaster. But fear not! This chapter is designed to help you manage the expectations of parents and any conflict that could arise from behaviour of pupils in your class.

The best word to describe a mother of a primary school child is 'lioness'. My head teacher often uses this analogy with parents when they are angry at a behaviour management decision that has been made. The analogy helps parents know that we understand why they may have reacted in a certain way to a certain situation. A mother's instinct is to protect her young, and if she feels that her cub (child) is being wronged, she can come bounding in on the hunt for her prey (the teacher or senior leader).

Not all parents are fearsome lionesses; others are more controlled and reflective, understanding that there are two sides to every story and seeking answers to ensure the matter is dealt with effectively. Consider them as more measured lionesses; protective, yes, but more willing to look at the whole picture. If the lion's share of parents (sorry...) were like this, dealing with incidents would be easy. But they are not, and you need to be prepared for that. The strategies discussed in this chapter will ensure you feel confident to tackle behaviour issues with parents.

What do parents think about behaviour management in school?

When my older sister was at primary school, she misbehaved. It's hard to believe, as the eldest children tend to be the ones who behave the best. When you get to child number three (me), you would expect the worst, but I was angelic…

The reason I tell you about my sister is twofold: 1) I like to brag about the fact that I was the most well-behaved of the three of us, and 2) her teacher slapped her on the leg for her bad behaviour.

Now, in fairness, this was in the mid 1970s, and smacking was part of a school discipline system, much as caning had been twenty years earlier. If you misbehaved, you got a smack; in my sister's case, on the back of the leg.

What do you think my mum's reaction was? Outrage? Demands to see the headteacher? Withdrawing my sister from school? No, none of the above. She actually agreed that physical punishment was the right way to manage my sister's behaviour and was happy for the teacher to use this method.

Fast-forward thirty years, and things are different. We no longer have 'smack books' or 'use the slipper', and rightly so. Even when I was at primary school, ten years later than my sister, smacking wasn't considered the 'done thing'. But let this story prompt you to think of how some of the parents of the children in your class were disciplined when they were children. My niece is currently at primary school age, so there may be some parents who had the same experience as my sister at school.

As a teacher, you will find that you get three types of parents:

- Those who rarely speak to you about your behaviour management style or systems, mainly because their child is beautifully behaved or because they are happy with the way you deal with things and support you wholeheartedly.

- Those who openly support your behaviour management style and expect you to be tough on their child (although hopefully not as tough as my sister's teacher was on her).

• Those who do not support your style. They think you are too strict, or in some cases, not strict enough.

You will get to know which parents match the above descriptions quite quickly, and most definitely by the time it's your first parents' evening. If you get the behaviour systems right from the start, you should find that your fair and consistent approach means you get hardly any negative comments from parents. More importantly, you will be able to confidently explain your behaviour management choices to the parents who make things more difficult by not always supporting you.

Why is it important to work alongside parents?

Working alongside parents ensures a more harmonious relationship for everyone involved, but more importantly, it means that the child will get the same response from home and from school. You can work together as a team and show high expectations for the individual child.

But working alongside parents is not always easy. Some parents are hard to reach and do not want to get actively involved with the school or engage with the teacher. In their eyes, the behaviour of their child is for you deal with, and they don't want to know about it.

Don't let these obstacles put you off. Don't let them be an excuse. Keep persevering and keep trying to build those links. If parents begin to feel that you are supportive and you are not always phoning to complain about their child, they may start to engage more with you.

Your relationships with parents will underpin the success of your behaviour management with the children. If parents have faith in what you are doing, they are more likely to impress upon their children the need to behave appropriately in school. Be supportive, not patronising, and make sure you recognise when things are going well.

How can you build up good communication with parents?

Be sure you speak to parents positively about their child. Parents often think that when they are in the playground at the end of the day and the teacher comes out and walks towards them, it must mean their child has been in trouble. Try to speak to parents about things their child has done very well, so that your conversations are not always a negative experience. Try a few phone calls to discuss positive behaviour or an excellent piece of work. Then those hard-to-reach parents will more readily speak to you about problematic incidents that have occurred.

It is important that you approach parents about positive contributions or behaviour that their child has displayed. You will certainly become more popular with them because of it, and if you are popular with the most popular parent, you're really on to a winner. Here are some other tips that could help you:

Be flexible about communication channels. If it's difficult to reach parents by phone, ask whether they would rather be contacted via email or using a home-school communication book.

Be proactive. If an incident occurs, be the first to make contact. Don't wait for parents to come to you. Be ready with the facts and explain how the incident was dealt with and why. In the case of persistent low-level behaviour problems, don't wait until the first parents' evening. Get the parents in early to discuss any problems that you are having.

Be approachable and available. Don't avoid meeting parents.

Invite them in and make sure you are giving them your undivided attention. Build relationships at the classroom door or in the playground in a more informal way.

Be discreet. Don't talk about a child's poor behaviour choices in the playground. It is embarrassing, and parents don't want everyone else hearing about their child's difficulties that day.

Keep a record of incidents. If behaviour is becoming an issue, make an appointment with a parent. Keep a diary of incidents that occur so that you have facts to support your concerns.

Apologise when needed. If you make a mistake, be a grown-up and apologise. A lioness's attitude will be less fearsome if you apologise. You can positively see the barriers coming down, the parent's face softening. Big tip here: don't use the phrase 'I'm sorry' — nobody has died. Use the phrase 'I apologise' — it is less emotional.

What if a parent doesn't back up your actions?

Unfortunately, parents can dispute your actions more often than we would like!

Some parents will take the teacher's word as gospel. These are the kinds of parents that you want to hug because you appreciate that they respect your choices.

Other parents, however, do not back up your decisions and can become quite sensitive about how you have dealt with a behaviour incident. You will soon know who these parents are — they will often be the first ones to speak to you early in the term when something happens to their child in the playground.

Instead of seeing these parents as a negative part of the job (and it is easy to do this), use it to develop an understanding of how best to deal with their concerns. The following tips will help you manage the responses of more sensitive parents:

Explain the situation. First, get the facts by investigating the incident with any children involved. As explained above, be the first to make contact with the parents. Then tell them that you have spoken to the children involved and you are able to explain both sides of what happened. Even if their child was the perpetrator, you need to be honest. Parents appreciate honesty and clarity. Don't waffle — make sure you deliver the facts.

Refer to the school's behaviour policy. Explain that you have followed school policy when dealing with the situation. Useful phrases are, 'The school expects the children to…' or 'The school rules encourage the children to…' Sometimes it is good to put 'the school' before 'I' — particularly if a parent is difficult to talk to.

Encourage parents to help you. Ask them to talk to the child about the incident that evening. Invite them to tell you if they learn anything that they think you should know or could shed further light on the incident.

Provide a sense of resolution. Reassure the parent that this issue has now been dealt with and that you are hoping the child has learned from the experience.

Emphasise learning. If the behaviour is persistent, talk about the effects that the behaviour is having on the child's learning and progress. Parents tend to listen more when you talk about how behaviour affects their child's learning rather than talking about it in general terms.

Get help when needed. If you still find that some parents are difficult to talk to, ask a senior member of staff to suggest the best way to approach that particular parent. You can also ask the member of staff to be present when you have the conversation.

Awkward conversations

On a few occasions, you may have to feed back something embarrassing to parents. For example, perhaps their child has used inappropriate language and you need to tell the parents exactly what was said.

Telling parents the details can be slightly mortifying — for them and for you! Remember to state the facts. In the case of inappropriate language, tell parents whether the child was overheard by other children or adults. If you feel worried about telling parents something embarrassing, ask for a more senior member of staff to talk to them with you.

The importance of empathy

Until I had children, I never really understood why parents reacted the way they did. Why did they cry at assemblies? Why did they jump up and down on the side-line at sports day, turning a lovely shade of puce in an attempt to get their child to cross the finish line first? Why were they so sensitive about every little thing?

Then I had my first son and, all of a sudden, I understood the bond between mother and child and it was like a wrecking ball in my gut. This is why parents did all those things and became like lionesses protecting their cubs.

I am not saying that you have to have children to understand a parent's perspective, but you do need an empathy with parents. You need to be able to think about the effects that getting negative feedback, sometimes frequently, might have on them. Talk to them sensitively, particularly if their child is getting into trouble regularly. Discuss any issues in private. Tell them how you are going to try to improve the behaviour of their child, such as by using reward charts or asking an educational psychologist for advice.

If you involve parents and include them in their child's behaviour, those parents who were once easily upset will now be listening to you and appreciating what you are doing.

Remember! Make a specific effort to contact these parents to tell them about the positives too! They will know that you are looking for the best qualities their child has, not just pointing out the poor decisions they can make.

Action steps

1. Be visible. Establish good relationships with parents from the word go. You can start on an informal level by interacting with them at the beginning or end of the day and getting to know them. Smile too!

2. Tell parents when an incident has happened. Don't leave it for the child to pass on.

3. Establish the facts about an incident before you speak to a parent. Talk to the children involved and make notes if you need to.

4. Explain things clearly and concisely — don't waffle. Use the school's behaviour policy to back up decisions you have made.

5. After an incident, let parents know that the child needs to move on from this experience. Tomorrow is a clean slate.

6. Encourage parents to speak to children about any behaviour issues, so that pupils realise that school and home work together.

Read on, Macduff!

The next chapter carries on with the theme of working in a partnership. We will look at other adults in the classroom and how they can have a positive impact on your behaviour management.

CHAPTER 9

Working with Your Teaching Assistant (TA)

Do you remember when you were younger and you wanted to ask an adult in your family if you could have some sweets or go out to play with your friends? Do you remember which adult you went to for this? Many children learn to ask the adult who is more likely to say, "yes" than "no". Children will try this not only with their family, but also with you and the other adults in your classroom. Make sure you develop a team approach to combat attempts from the children to play one adult off against the other.

What are the benefits of the team approach to behaviour management?

Children are savvy creatures. They can smell out weakness like a dog can smell sausages in a butcher's shop. They can also identify when adults don't have a united approach. Unless you and the other adults in the room adopt the same behaviour management style, the children are going to know that one person is a more of a pushover than the other.

Working as a team has many benefits, but consistency has to be the main one. The children have to know that whomever they go to, they are going to get the same response. Situations are going to be handled in the same way, and the same procedures and systems are going to be followed.

Achieving a team approach will take some planning on your part.

You will need to discuss your behaviour management strategies with your TA before pupils arrive in September. Give your TA the idea behind the SIMPLE approach and the systems that you are planning to set up. As an NQT, you are in a good position as the behaviour policy will be fresh in your mind, as you must read it before you start.

After reading the policy, have a conversation with your TA. Talk about the school's approach to behaviour management, as well as your own approach that you hope to adopt in the classroom. Being clear from the first day will certainly help things in the long run.

Within the classroom, the children will have consistency and will know where they stand. The children will feel safe and well-supported in a classroom where everyone delivers the same message and uses the same systems. It can be unsettling for children, and even downright worrying for some, if they don't think that behaviour is managed in the same way by everyone.

A final benefit is for your own sanity. You may sometimes come home and feel like you want to remove your vocal chords, just so you don't have to hear your voice anymore. If it is only *your* voice, *your* insistence, *your* expectations, then the day becomes longer than is comfortable to bear and the children switch off.

I don't expect that you have someone in your room all day, every day — and I don't think you should. But when you do have a TA in your room, you need to use each other to manage the class. You need to know that if you are working with a focus group and there is some unrest in the class, your TA will manage it so that you can work. The same goes for when the TA has a focus group and you are floating around. You can rely on one another.

How can a team approach be used effectively?

As well as talking about your own principles and ideas, ask the TA what has worked well with the classes that he or she has been in.

That way you'll ensure that the TA's opinions and ideas are part of the process and that you value them. Discuss options and come up with a style that you can both commit to.

Some teaching assistants are less confident when managing class behaviour. If that's true of your TA, you will need to discuss how to tackle this issue. Explain that you are happy for the TA to manage low-level disruption and that you don't see it as purely your job to do so. You might suggest that your TA get some training or observe another TA who manages behaviour effectively. Many TAs feel they become more confident when working alongside a teacher who is more skilled at behaviour management; they pick up tips and tricks they can try.

If you think the teacher is the only one responsible for behaviour management in the classroom, it is time you have a long, hard look at yourself and your belief system.

Some teachers think the role of 'behaviour manager' is one that only the class teacher can fill. I think that's ridiculous. You may not agree with me, and that is your prerogative. But ignore the capabilities of your TA at your peril. Communication and a team approach between teacher and TA are crucial in all aspects of the job, particularly when you are managing the behaviour of thirty children. Don't feel as though letting your TA take on some of the behaviour management role means you are not able to do the job effectively. It just makes your life easier, as the workload (and stress!) can be shared.

Ensure that both you and the TA sign the class contract for behaviour, to show that you are willing to stick to the systems and rules that have been put in place. The children will see that both of you are taking the contract seriously and that you want to be a part of the class team.

What if your TA doesn't stick to the class rules?

This problem can be a difficult one. If you have thirty children who find it hard to follow the rules, you don't need anyone extra added into the mix. A TA who doesn't follow the rules can make behaviour management harder than it needs to be. Here are two approaches you can try when trying to manage, what could be, a tricky situation.

Using a light touch

Sometimes issues can be resolved fairly painlessly with a light touch. That means tackling the problem head on, but in a way that doesn't appear to be too confrontational.

For example, suppose your TA calls out answers or ideas when you are doing a whole class activity or input. This can be frustrating when you have worked really hard to encourage the children to respond to your request for 'hands up' or when you are asking individual, targeted pupils for answers.

The next time the TA calls out an answer, you could say something like, 'Now Mr X, you know that in this class we put our hands up when we want to share ideas!' Give Mr X a smile so that he doesn't take offence, and the light touch will probably work.

Having a direct conversation

Sometimes you might need to have a more direct, and potentially more difficult, conversation with the TA.

The outcome and success of a difficult conversation depends on the strength of the relationship underneath. If you have a good working relationship, then a difficult conversation should, in theory, be easier. The TA will know that your concern is not coming from a malicious place, but from a professional one.

The following method can be used with great success, as it

provides a structure that is easily adaptable. You will need to imagine the conversation as a diamond shape. There are three steps to it:

1. State the Need to Talk (the top of the diamond): The best way to structure a conversation that might be awkward is to state the awkwardness at the very start. Tell the TA that the two of you need to talk, but that it might be a difficult conversation. For example, you might say, "Could we have a chat about something? It might be a bit awkward, but it is important that we have it." When the TA knows that what you're going to say might be difficult to hear, it won't come as a bolt out of the blue. Reassure the TA that this feeling of awkwardness extends to you too, but that hopefully, by having this conversation, you will be able to move forward and continue working well together.

2. State the Problem (the widest points of the diamond): Suppose the TA shouts at children when they are not following the class rules. You have worked hard to develop a culture of mutual respect and to lead by example, but it isn't working.

You could approach the problem by saying, "I have noticed that we have quite a different approach to dealing with the Tim's difficult behaviour. I was wondering whether we could discuss an approach we could both use to ensure consistency for him." As this example shows, throughout your conversation you should speak in a way that is respectful, not condescending or patronising.

3. Suggest the Solution and Summarise (the bottom point of the diamond): Having spoken about the problem, suggest a solution. Be sure it is a team approach — something that you can both work on. That way you won't imply that only the TA needs to change. For example, "I have noticed that Tim responds well when [describe a behaviour technique]. I wondered if we could use that approach for a couple of weeks and see how he responds?" Also ask for the TA's opinion: "Is there anything you know works well for him?" Once you agree on a solution, summarise what has been said.

Then suggest that you follow up at a later date, such as in a fortnight, to review the behaviour and the management strategies that you both used.

A key principle to this kind of conversation is that you want to ensure consistency for the class. Always put the children or an individual pupil at the centre of decision-making — no one should argue with that!

What if, despite trying to resolve differences using a direct conversation, consistency still isn't in place? In that case, ask your mentor or a senior leader to help you.

The benefits of good relationships

I want to share an example of how to develop a great relationship with a teaching assistant. Hopefully it will show you how important this can be when managing children's behaviour.

One of my teaching assistants, Jacqui, is fantastic. She has a wealth of knowledge about all things to do with special educational needs and disabilities, which I greatly admire and respect. If anyone needs an idea for an intervention, Jacqui is your lady.

Last year, we had to take on a class due to the teacher's long-term sickness. This class had experienced a number of teachers and teaching styles, none of which they had responded to particularly well. Jacqui and I knew the class, and we knew we had to put a system in place to try to ensure consistency in behaviour.

There was already another lovely TA in that class, Hannah, whom we wanted to get on board to ensure a team approach. These were the strategies we put in place that worked well:

• We understood that all of us could take on the role of behaviour manager. I am not precious, and whilst I was the deputy head, I saw our roles as equal in this process. The children needed to know that all of the adults were 'singing from the same hymn sheet' and that our responses would be the same.

- We established clear boundaries and rules. The class had got into a habit of shouting out, and that needed to stop, so we focused on that behaviour the most.

- We set high expectations — ones we agreed on at the start, so that we all knew what we were striving for.

- We made sure we understood any special educational needs or disabilities in the class, particularly those related to behaviour.

- We talked to each other and gave each other feedback. For example, what had any of us noticed about a particular child? Were there specific triggers that would lead to certain behaviour choices? Did X and Y need to move apart from one another to ensure a better working environment?

Whilst they were still a challenge at times, the children appreciated the high expectations and boundaries that were put in place. This experience emphasised to me the importance of working with my teaching assistants to develop a class that is well managed.

Mistakes

The main mistakes you can make when trying to work with your TA on behaviour management are:

- Developing 'good cop, bad cop' roles. We just want 'consistent cop'!

- Not establishing what the systems are going to be prior to the class starting in September.

- Not establishing a team approach to behaviour management. If there is inconsistency, children will learn which adult to come to in order to get away with something.

• Being precious about who manages behaviour. All adults in the class do, so get over any feelings of negativity towards this or you'll be a missing out on an effective approach.

• Failing to address inconsistent approaches to behaviour management. Use the 'diamond shape' to help you structure difficult conversations.

Action steps

Hopefully I have been able to convince you that the team approach is the best approach. Don't succumb to any of the mistakes that are listed above. Instead, think about:

1. Organising a meeting with your TA to discuss behaviour management strategies prior to the term starting.

2. Explain the systems that you wish to use and your desire for consistency.

3. If a TA isn't following the class rules themselves, use the diamond structure to make sure you have an effective, proactive conversation.

4. Remember! Consistent systems mean consistent behaviour.

Read on, Macduff!

The next chapter will look at how to manage more difficult situations with pupils who may have behaviour needs, or — using the terminology of the current code of practice — social, emotional and mental health needs (SEMH). You will be able to use the techniques and strategies described in that chapter to help you diffuse more difficult situations and feel more confident when they arise.

CHAPTER 10

Challenging Behaviour

Most undesirable behaviour in mainstream schools tends to be the low-level type that occurs on a daily basis. Not a day will go past when you don't have to manage something associated with a low-level disruption, be it reminding children how to walk around the school or waiting for the class to be quiet so that you can give them a set of instructions.

However, there will be occasions when the behaviour that you are trying to manage is more than just low-level. Reading this chapter will help you feel confident in tackling such behaviour when it arises. This type of behaviour can come in various forms:

- Physical aggression towards another child or an adult

- Verbal aggression

- Refusal to do what they have been asked to do, such as come off the playground

- Bullying

- Deliberately disrupting lessons, such as by throwing things across the classroom and distracting others

Sometimes these behaviours are a result of an underlying difficulty that needs to be managed sensitively and carefully, possibly following a behaviour plan that has been created by a senior member of staff (usually the SENCO). This situation is covered further in Chapter 10.

Often, physical or verbal aggression can take place due to a simple disagreement, such as over a football game. Using the rules discussed in this chapter should help to diffuse this type of behaviour and manage it effectively.

The most important thing to take from this chapter is that children will respond to a crisis situation in one of three ways:

- Fight

- Flight

- Freeze

This isn't a conscious choice that the child is making. Rather, it is linked to the way that the human brain has developed. It goes all the way back to the evolution of man, so there is no point getting too stressed about it.

Moreover, in the peak of anxiety, children's senses will shut down and they won't be able to hear you. Giving them a big lecture is pointless when they are stressed and not able to regulate their emotions.

What to do in a situation that is getting beyond your control

Stick to the rules below and you should find yourself managing more difficult situations with confidence and success.

Stay calm

Sounds easy, doesn't it? But believe me, it's not — particularly if a child has been rude to you or even attempted to physically harm you. You must remember that you are the adult in this situation. Remaining as calm as you can enables you to think with some measure of clarity and control. Also consider that some children thrive on the response they get to their behaviour. As much as you may want to, don't shout or raise your voice. Don't get into a child's 'personal space', either, as the child will often see that as confrontational.

Seek assistance from another adult

An additional adult, particularly one from the senior team, is useful for two reasons:

Supporting you in managing the situation. This support might be in the form of taking responsibility for the situation or providing you with the confidence you need to continue.

Witnessing the encounter. It is a sad fact that some children will fabricate what has happened in order to get themselves out of potential trouble. Remember, the human brain is programmed to think in the 'fight, flight, or freeze' capacity here, so children will do or say whatever they think will get them out of the situation they are in. Another adult who witnessed the incident can make sure there is an accurate record of events, should the need arise.

To get adult support, ask another child to alert other adults who are nearby, such as in the playground or neighbouring classrooms, or to get help from the school office.

Allow time for the child to calm down

Don't demand that the child with challenging behaviour respond to you right away. They are not in the right 'place' to do this and it can only antagonise the situation. If you can show an understanding of this, you are far more likely to eventually get the response you want from them, when they have regulated their emotions successfully.

Offer options

In this situation, you would give the pupil two choices:

Option 1. Jack agrees to come with you now, calmly, to a quiet place to calm down before discussions take place.

Option 2. If Jack chooses not to go with you, explain to him that two adults will remove him from the situation. I am not implying that Jack will be dragged off, kicking and screaming, to a room to be locked away. I am suggesting the use of 'positive handling', a technique that has to be used in schools when the behaviour is so challenging that it poses a risk to the child or their peers. Positive handling requires staff to be trained in various techniques that ensure they can move a child safely to a space where they can calm themselves down. NQTs should not be expected to use positive handling. If for any reason you find that you are required to use this technique, you must request and complete the appropriate training to ensure you keep yourself, and the child, safe.

The most important thing to remember here is that in all schools, it is always used as a last resort.

Explain the two options to Jack and suggest he makes the right decision.

Praise the child

If Jack does choose to come with you to a quiet place, briefly give him praise for making the appropriate choice. If you have promised to give him time to self-regulate his emotions, you need to deliver on this promise. As much as you might want to talk about what has happened, give Jack some space. Doing so shows that you respect him, and he will respect you all the more in return.

Record what the child says

When the time is right, sit down with Jack and write a record of what he thinks happened. Explain that you are going to get the other side of the story from any other pupils involved, and make sure you do.

Apply sanctions

Calmly explain that due to his behaviour choices, sanctions will need to be put in place. Follow your school's policy on what those sanctions are and make sure that they are followed through.

By following the steps listed above, you should find that the children see you as a fair but firm teacher who handles situations calmly. They will feel safe and confident to talk to you because you are treating them with respect.

Why is it important to stick to school policies?

School policies provide you with the systems that you are expected to put in place. In addition to the behaviour policy, be sure to read the positive handling or restraint policy, as it will give you guidelines should you need them.

These policies are there to protect you as well as to guide you. If you stick to them, there should be no reason why mistakes are made. Sometimes parents might question why you made a particular decision, and it is very helpful if you can say that you were simply following the school's policy. If parents have any issues with the policy itself, they can take that up with the senior team.

If you don't stick to school policies, things can become difficult and complaints can be made that need to be investigated. If you are ever unsure of how to handle a tricky situation, seek advice from your mentor or a senior leader. Better still, ask one of them to assist you in the situation, and then you can see the best way to handle it.

How can you stop incidents from happening?

The secret to preventing behaviour incidents is to know your children. Every Friday morning in my school, as part of our staff briefing, we discuss children that we all need to be aware of, including those who are displaying more challenging behaviour.

Some children in the school may have behaviour plans, and it is useful for you to know the best way to handle situations involving them. You will be on playground duty, after all, and this is the prime time for incidents to take place!

For children who do display challenging behaviour, you will need to know what is happening in their lives at any particular time. Are they going through a parental separation? Is the family facing eviction? Does the child have to cope with a sibling with additional needs? Think back to the 'Iceberg Model' — the behaviour we see is only the tip of the iceberg. Identifying what is going on underneath is important and can be described as 'triggers.' A trigger is something that happens frequently that leads to undesirable behaviour. Examples of triggers are changes in routine (especially for children with special educational needs or disabilities), anxiety around work, or playing with particular children. These are not excuses for challenging behaviour, but they definitely can be a reason for it. Knowing the triggers for children in your class can help you identify situations that are likely to cause a negative change in behaviour. If you see things beginning to 'bubble' for a particular child, intervene there and then. Don't wait for it all to explode, as by then the child is past the point of negotiation and you will need to wait for the child to calm down before resolving anything.

Distraction is another effective way to take the heat out of a situation, particularly with younger children. Simply start talking about something else and let the children shift their attention. Humour can also be a good way to diffuse a potential incident. You will know your children and what will work with them and what won't. For children with autism, humour could be the worst approach; they might respond better to distraction or taking them out of the situation.

Get to know your children, and you may be able to stop difficult situations from happening in the first place.

Remember the key pearl of wisdom: All behaviour is communication

What if you are threatened by a pupil?

Being threatened by a pupil may well affect you quite deeply. It will certainly stay with you throughout your teaching career, and you will always be able to recall the incident when telling colleagues or friends. These incidents stick with you for a reason. They affect you emotionally, even if you think you are quite a tough person. There is no shame in feeling upset or distressed by what has happened. Acknowledge those feelings and do something about them. This may mean speaking to your mentor, a member of your school's pastoral team (if they have one) or, if necessary, arranging a counselling session through the local authority's HR department.

If you are on the receiving end of a child's outburst, tell a senior member of staff so that parents can be contacted as appropriate. As soon as possible, write down what happened as accurately as you can. Date and sign this record of the event.

This might be difficult to believe, but children are often more anxious about facing you again after an incident than you are about seeing them. They feel a sense of embarrassment and also, hopefully, some remorse. Make seeing you again as painless as possible for them. As much as you are feeling hurt about what happened, once the incident has been dealt with, you *must* move on and give children an opportunity to redeem themselves. Don't hold a grudge.

If the problem is a recurring one, it may be the time to involve your SENCO or outside professionals. They can look into the behaviour further and to give you strategies to support this child appropriately.

Example

Prior to teaching a particular class, I had been made aware of one boy's tendency to be physically aggressive towards the teachers and the deputy head. The night before I was due to start teaching him, I remember worrying about what I should do if this boy tried to be physically aggressive with me. I knew that he had previously punched members of staff and that the class had been evacuated when he had cornered the deputy head and repeatedly hit her.

I think 'nervous' is an understatement.

I knew that I needed to know what this boy's triggers were, as well as ensure that I set the boundaries high. The advice I had been given regarding the best way to manage him was varied and didn't give me a lot of confidence.

After a few days, I realised that the boy had very low self-esteem and his attitude about his work was poor. He often used his aggressive or disruptive behaviour to avoid doing the work that he had been asked to do and would become very defensive if I tried to discuss it with him. I was also aware that his family life was difficult, as his parents struggled to manage his very difficult behaviour. His TA and I worked through strategies to help him manage his anxieties, using the support provided by our attached educational psychologist.

I also began to realise that the boy had a wicked sense of humour and that using humour to diffuse situations worked well. So did giving him space and time to calm down. He responded well to both of these initiatives and knew that I would not demand he speak to me until he felt calmer. He liked the fact that I had expectations for him, and once he had tested those boundaries and found that I did not budge, he felt safe and valued in the classroom. He liked the fact that I spoke to him 'on a level' and didn't talk down to him.

These positive results didn't stop me being anxious about the possibilities of what this boy could do. But in the end, I enjoyed teaching him, as it gave me so many more skills to manage difficult behaviour effectively.

Get to know your children and what they do and do not like.

Work with outside professionals and try the strategies they suggest; they are specialists in their field.

Mistakes

The most common mistakes that teachers and other adults can make when managing challenging behaviour are:

Rushing about in a state of panic. You need to remain calm and reassure the other children that the situation is being dealt with in a controlled way. No footsteps should be heard running down a corridor unless there is a genuine, life-threatening emergency.

Ignoring the additional needs of particular pupils. If they have a behaviour plan, follow it. If the plan suggests you give them space to calm down, do it. These plans are put together by professionals, so make sure you stick to them.

Reacting in an angry way. Even if this is your initial response, do your best to remain calm. Shouting isn't going to make the situation any better and will just add to children's anxiety levels.

Action steps

• Stay calm – remember that you need to be in control of the situation.

• Seek assistance from another adult – it is best that there are two of you to manage any really challenging behaviour.

• Don't make demands for a response – respect the fact that the child may not be ready to talk and asking him or her to do so, may antagonise the situation further.

- Give the child two choices – make sure you explain both choices clearly and calmly. The child needs to be aware that there is the possibility of staff assisting them to move to a separate space to regulate themselves, but that it would be easier for everybody if they came voluntarily. I normally use the phrase, "to keep you safe, I will have to ask another member of staff to come and help me to move you somewhere quieter."

- Praise the child appropriately – if he or she does come voluntarily, don't overdo the praise but make sure that you thank them for coming and say how pleased you are that they made that choice. Remember, at this point, keep the language simple and save any further discussions for later.

- Record what happened – once the child feels able to talk (and I always ask them if they are ready), explain to them that you need to write down what happened before they became upset or angry, as it is important to hear their side of things. Do explain that you will need to ask other children for their explanations and once you have done that, you will let them all know the outcome.

Read on, Macduff!

This chapter has briefly mentioned how special educational needs can affect a child's behaviour. The next chapter will look at this issue in more detail. It will help you feel confident in managing the different types of needs in your class, and you will also learn when it might be a good time to involve your school's SENCO.

CHAPTER 11

Behaviour and SEND

The 2015 Code of Practice for special educational needs and disability (SEND) highlights, more than ever before, the importance of the teacher's responsibility for all children in the class and the progress that they make. Historically, the provision and progress of children with SEND had largely been left to the special educational needs coordinator (SENCO) and, more often than not, the TAs who took these children out for 'corridor learning'. Most teachers had therefore been unaware of how these children were progressing on a day-to-day basis, and the responsibility had fallen with the TA.

But times are changing. The code has recognised that teachers may not be fully aware of, or be fully managing, the needs of the SEND pupils, including their behaviour management. Interestingly, the code has taken out the word 'behaviour' and replaced it with 'social, emotional, and mental health' (SEMH). It has put an emphasis on looking at the underlying causes of a child's behaviour, rather than just focusing on the behaviour itself.

Therefore, it is now more important for teachers to have a good understanding of the different types of SEND, particularly those that are commonly linked to SEMH. Unfortunately, teacher training does not place an adequate focus on this need, and more and more teachers are entering classrooms without the appropriate training or understanding of SEND.

Now this is an enormous topic, more likely to be a book in itself, so I won't go into too much detail about the types of needs you may experience in your teaching career. But you need to be aware of some of them and feel confident to manage them, or at least know whom to go to if you require further support.

The key person for you in this situation is the SENCO rather than your mentor. Your mentor might be the first point of contact if you are struggling with a child's behaviour, but if the behaviour is at all related to SEND, make contact with the SENCO.

Traditionally, teachers would approach the SENCO and describe the problem that they were having with a particular pupil. They would then ask, "What do you suggest I do about it?" I know this because I have been a SENCO for the last four years! As a result of the most recent Code of Practice, SENCOs are now encouraged to respond with, "Well, what have you already done?" You are expected to try some ideas out first and come to the SENCO when these ideas did not work as well as you had hoped.

This chapter will give you some strategies to try so that you feel confident to go to your SENCO. The SENCO can then further develop your ideas or ensure that you meet with an appropriate external professional, such as an educational psychologist, to guide you and support you further.

What are the different types of SEND that affect behaviour?

There are many types of SEND that affect the behaviour of a child and for many different reasons. Here are some of the most commonly occurring conditions that can lead to more difficult or challenging behaviour.

Neurodevelopmental conditions

Autism often leads to difficult behaviour. Children with autism do not 'see' the world the way we do. They often struggle with social skills, literal understanding and expression, poor speech development (some with no speech at all), obsessive behaviours, anxiety, and sensory difficulties. Their behaviour can often be quite 'explosive' and physically aggressive. They need routine and simple language, at the very least.

Attention deficit disorder (ADD) and attention deficit hyperactivity disorder (ADHD) affect children's concentration, ability to organise themselves, and anxiety levels. Children with ADHD always appear 'on the go' and find it difficult to wind down. As a result, their sleep is often affected, which makes them tired and more prone to finding concentration difficult. They can be physically aggressive to peers, often because they are quite boisterous and overexcited. Some children are medicated to support their needs.

Dyspraxia used to be referred to as 'clumsy child syndrome'. Children with this condition have difficulty with fine and gross motor skills, which in turn can lead to frustration and anger. They can dislike writing and recording large amounts of work, which can lead to defiance and a poor attitude towards learning. They can also find organising themselves and their belongings very difficult. They will often return to the classroom several times at the end of day, as they have left their items behind.

Remember that no child ever has a 'pure' condition. Children often have co-occurring difficulties that affect their learning and their day-to-day lives. For example, a child with Autism can also be dyspraxic.

Other conditions

Speech and language difficulties can affect either expressive or receptive language, or both. That is, children can be frustrated by not being able to express themselves efficiently or by not understanding what they have been asked to do. They can also struggle with sequencing events, so they might not be able to recall and explain what happened during an incident.

Global developmental delay affects all areas of development, including behaviour. Children with this condition may act and behave in quite an immature way and may not be able to explain their behaviour. They can often be quite physically aggressive because they become frustrated with not being able to express themselves appropriately or make other children understand what they want.

Pathological Demand Avoidance is becoming more common and is considered to be part of the autism spectrum. Many of the difficulties mirror the social interaction needs of children with autism, but they are driven to avoid demands and expectations. This is because they have an anxiety based need to be in control. Their obsessive behaviour is often linked to people, which can make this difficult to manage within the classroom, as other children can find this overwhelming.

Why is it important to treat these children differently?

Think about this quote from Thomas Jefferson: 'There is nothing so unequal as the equal treatment of unequals.'

Children with SEND are not choosing to behave in the way that they do. Quite often, they are not able to explain exactly why they made the behaviour choices that they did. You need to have a solid understanding of their particular special needs so that you can respond appropriately.

I am not suggesting that you lower your expectations or that you allow behaviour that is unacceptable. What is crucial is an understanding of 'why'. Ros Blackburn, who is an adult with autism, speaks about her life with the condition and provides many thought-provoking ideas. She feels it is important for people to understand that her autism is 'often the reason, but not an excuse.'

SEND difficulties are the reason a child may behave in a certain way, but these difficulties shouldn't be an excuse. If a child with autism hurts another child, we understand the reason (the autistic child struggles with appropriate social skills), but he or she shouldn't be allowed to hurt others without an appropriate consequence. The child needs to be made aware of hurting the other child and apologise for doing so. It might take a lot of intervention to enable this apology to happen, but it does need to happen. The child needs to develop social skills to function later in life, so this is when you would think about strategies to help with this, such as a social story. This would be written under the guidance of the SENCO or therapist.

Again, this goes back to knowing your children and supporting them appropriately. If you don't take the time to get to know the triggers for your child with autism, or the areas that your child with speech and language difficulties finds hard to express, you will not be able to manage that child's behaviour to the best of your ability.

How to manage SEND behaviour in the classroom and work with the SENCO

The SENCO is the person in the school who has the responsibility for the progress and attainments of the SEND pupils. You will go to the SENCO when you have tried some strategies of your own and they are still not working. Use the SENCO's expertise and don't be afraid to ask for help. Managing certain types of SEND can be very challenging, and you need to make sure that you are able to do this effectively.

If you have been told that certain strategies work for identified pupils, do yourself a favour and try them. Don't decide that this will be the year that your pupil with autism works within a small group if she is used to having her own workstation and working on her own. Don't provide excuses like, "we don't have space for a workstation" or "'I thought we might try and see how she gets on within a group." Yes, ideally that is the aim, but these things take time. Pupils with autism will already be anxious enough about starting in a new classroom with a new teacher, so taking away their 'safe space' could be catastrophic for them.

Keep your high expectations for behaviour. Remember my Year 6 pupil who had particularly aggressive behaviour? On my very first day, he decided to challenge the boundaries by making continuous animal noises, similar to those found on a farm. He was deliberately testing me and, although I had been told to simply ignore these distractions, I felt that I needed to address it with him. No one else was allowed to make those noises, so he needed to know that those expectations stretched to him too. Pick your battles with some children (you'll know who they are), but don't let the SEND become an excuse for poor behaviour.

Ask other teachers about particular pupils; spend time understanding what works well for them and what doesn't. You'll develop your own strategies as the years go on, but don't be gung-ho about it and throw out old strategies with disregard.

Listen to the external professionals too. They often have a wealth of knowledge that you can use with particular children. Usually their advice works. If it doesn't work, say so.

Put the child first in all decision-making. Don't struggle with a strategy that is clearly not working and is stressful for both you and the child. You will probably find that strategies that don't work for one child may well work for another child in years to come.

Embrace the challenge, but seek support for it. Your confidence in managing children's behaviour will only improve because of it.

What if the behaviour is becoming too much?

There will be times when you feel as though the behaviour of a pupil is becoming too much for you to manage. It could also be affecting the learning of other children, as well as the dynamics of the class.

This would be the time to seek specific help and request a

meeting with your SENCO. Don't think that you are failing because you aren't managing a child's behaviour as well as you would like or as well as other teachers have in the past. Perhaps the child's needs are changing as he or she grows, so the school will need to rethink how best to meet those needs.

Schools can tap into a wealth of external advice to provide the help you need for a particular pupil. Your school's educational psychologist will probably be the first port of call. The EP will be able to not only consult with you about the behaviours the child is displaying, but also devise strategies to help. Often the EP will come into class to observe the child and understand the problems more thoroughly.

If a child's behaviour is becoming too much to handle, speak up and ask for support. Don't be a hero — you'll only suffer because of it, and so will the rest of the class.

Review meetings

The 2015 Code requires that all pupils who are on the school's SEND register must have termly review meetings. These review meetings will involve parents, adults who work with the child in school and possibly external professionals. Come to these meetings prepared to discuss not only the progress of the child academically, but also any strategies that are working to manage the child's behaviour. Remember, not all SEND will manifest itself with SEMH needs, so this won't be applicable to every review meeting.

Strategies that worked with SEND pupils in previous years may suddenly stop working, which makes your job more difficult. The reasons can vary. Perhaps as these children get older, they want to start challenging the boundaries that have been in place since they were young. Or their needs may change over time due to their condition.

If strategies no longer seem effective, it may be necessary to hold an interim review or Team Around the Child (TAC) meeting. Sit down as a team (with all adults involved with the child, including the SENCO) and discuss how the child's needs have changed. Involve the parents (who may have also noticed a change too). Discuss the advice you need in order to move forward. Remember that planning effective behaviour management is not just one person's job, but a team approach. Coming together to discuss a child is very powerful, as it ensures all areas are covered and that there is an agreed strategy going forward.

Your school might be very proactive and have frequent Team Around the Child (TAC) meetings to discuss pupils, as described above. If not, why not suggest to your mentor that you have a meeting like this, in order for discussions to take place. Be an initiator and look for solutions. Your practice will improve, and you will make a good impression on the senior team as someone who is keen to seek answers and move your own professional development forward.

Mistakes

Here are mistakes that teachers often make with regard to SEND:

- Not understanding a particular need. If you don't know enough about a pupil's particular condition, read about it and improve your knowledge.

- Not telling anyone when you are struggling with trying to manage difficult behaviour. No martyrs allowed!

- Not taking on board the suggestions and strategies of others that have been successful.

- Not reading a child's Statement or Education, Health and Care Plan (EHCP) to understand his or her needs more fully. You'd be surprised at how many teachers don't do this.

- Failing to work with your SEND pupils at least twice a week in the classroom. It is no longer acceptable to simply ask the TA to work with them. You must plan to spend some time with them yourself. This will also build up your relationships with your SEND pupils, which will help with managing their behaviour.

- Failing to build a good relationship with parents. It is important to have regular, informal conversations with parents of SEND pupils to ensure that regular communication happens between home and school. Another good way to ensure this happens is to set up a 'home-school diary' that both teachers and parents can write in each day, to notify each other of anything significant or to give general feedback on behaviour throughout the day.

Action steps

1. Before starting a new class, read any notes about children with SEND. These may include a Statement or an Education and Health Care Plan, as well as notes from previous teachers, other professionals, or review meetings.

2. Write down the child's condition and do some research. Some children may have a SEND difficulty that you have not encountered before.

3. Talk to the SENCO about ideas for keeping behaviour management consistent with the previous year (for example, providing a work station for an autistic child, if that worked well previously).

4. Discuss strategies with the other adults in the class to ensure a consistent approach.

5. If strategies used in the past are no longer working, ask for a TAC meeting to discuss possible changes in the child's needs and to develop a team approach.

6. Ensure you have regular communication with the child's parents. As with any child, make sure this is not just in the form of negative comments. Point out the positives too. Set up a home-school book so that there is regular communication between home and school.

7. Attend review meetings or TAC meetings with books and information about progress. Talk confidently about what works well for the child and what you think are still areas for development, particularly with behaviour. When working with external professionals, come with examples of situations when behaviour has been a challenge to manage.

8. Be confident that you can manage a child's SEND behaviour needs, but ask for advice when you need it.

Read on, Macduff!

This chapter has been a whistle-stop tour of SEND and behaviour. There will always be SEND difficulties that you have not experienced before, but learning to manage them will only add to your repertoire. If you want to read more about a particular condition, ask your SENCO for some books that could help you.

The next chapter provides sound advice if you feel that you are not coping and addresses how to ensure that you are looking after yourself when things get tough.

CHAPTER 12

Help! I'm Not Coping

During your NQT year, your health and well-being is of paramount importance. Your body will need to battle against all sorts of things that come your way, including germs and bugs that pass through the school, wiping out nearly everyone in their wake. You will also face grumpy parents, deadlines from the senior team, and a class full of expectant pupils every day. Behaviour management will be just the icing on the cake, particularly during the autumn term.

Why the autumn? This is when your systems will need setting up and sticking to. Spring and summer terms tend to be less behaviour management heavy (ideally!), as the children have gotten to know your style and your rules. The autumn is long, dark, and full of illness. The build-up to Christmas can also cause some children to make poor behaviour choices because the structure of the days sometimes goes awry.

So strap yourself in for the bumpy ride that is the start of the new academic year, but keep your eyes open on this ride. You will need to recognise any signs that you are not coping with the behaviour management of your class and do something about it.

What are the signs that you may not be coping with managing your class?

Many teachers improve their behaviour management with time and experience. But you're an NQT — you have only your teaching practices to compare to. Even then, they weren't your class; you were simply following the behaviour management rules of someone else.

So when you have your own class and you try to put in the SIMPLE approach to develop your own behaviour management strategy, how can you be sure that you are doing it right? How can you know if you're not managing your class well? Look out for these signs and reflect on them:

- You find yourself changing your behaviour management strategies every week, without giving them time to embed.

- You feel genuinely frustrated at the choices the children are making.

- Your voice level is rising — you are shouting at the children or overreacting to the small things that happen.

- Low-level disruption is continuing despite the systems you have put in place. For example, the children talk over you or don't follow the morning routine you have developed.

- Your mentor has observed your class and noted that behaviour management is an area for development.

This is certainly not an exhaustive list, but these are the more common signs that teachers can experience. Be mindful of them and don't ignore that they are happening. Your awareness of your teaching is going to come down to one very important strategy: reflection.

Why is it important to reflect on how you are managing behaviour?

Self-reflection is important for teachers. It helps you develop an awareness of strategies and techniques that work well, as well as those that don't. But here's the thing. Your self-reflection needs to be honest. Reflecting honestly on your teaching is crucial so that you can constantly improve and evolve your practice.

You know those teachers who still teach the same lessons in the same style with the same behaviour management strategies, year after year after year? Don't strive to be one of those teachers! Strive to be a teacher who tries new things, reflects on lessons, and uses your experiences to inform your practice. If a behaviour experience has proved to be very difficult, see it as a learning opportunity. You might not feel like reflecting on it like that straight away, but do seek to use it as a learning experience.

If, when you reflect, you realise that your behaviour management is not going as well as you planned or would have liked, you need to do something about it. Burying your head in the sand is not the answer; it will only make the situation worse.

How can you help yourself?

Part of reflecting on your practice is to think about how you can help yourself improve. No one is born as an outstanding teacher. We learn and grow into that by constantly refining what we do. Here are some top tips for improving your behaviour management by helping yourself:

Watch others. Learn from experienced members of staff. If you know that some of them handle behaviour management really well, ask to observe them and take notes. What do they do that works well? What could you adopt in your own classroom? After observing them, ask if they can meet with you to discuss the strategies they use and answer your questions. Get them a little something for their time.

Ask senior leaders for support. Is there anyone on the senior team that you could ask for advice? I would go for the deputy head or your mentor (this may be one and the same person). Ask for a dedicated meeting time — don't try and sort it as you pass the person in the corridor.

Read books (like this one!). Look for books that can help you understand children's behaviour, including anything that gives you information on why children find it difficult to express themselves appropriately. Plenty of behaviour management books are out there. When I started out, I read *Getting the Buggers to Behave* by Sue Cowley, it gave me lots of tips and ideas to try.

Exercise. This may sound like a strange thing to put in a behaviour management book, but it is important. If you have a particularly challenging class or child, give yourself time to clear your head. Exercise releases endorphins, which make it more likely you'll be able to deal with incidents rationally and calmly. Even if you simply go for a thirty-minute walk every day, you will be amazed at how much better you feel and how much more ably you can tackle challenges.

Practise work-life balance. Yes, I know, I heard you snort in disbelief. Many NQTs make the mistake of not prioritising their life over their work. You need to ensure that you get time away from work and from thinking about work. Is there a hobby that you enjoy? Can you schedule time to see your friends? The more refreshed you are and the more time you spend thinking about something other than difficult behaviour, the more ready you will feel to manage it properly. Some teachers say that they don't let themselves work past 9 p.m. *9 p.m.?* You shouldn't let yourself work past 6 p.m., or for more than a few hours on the weekend. It takes practice, but you will get there in the end.

Sleep. Getting enough sleep might seem like a distant memory, but sleep is vitally important for physical and mental health and well-being. If you have adequate sleep, you are able to manage challenging behaviour with more ease. If you are tired, you are likely to be irritable, which can cause you to make decisions that you wouldn't normally make and give sanctions that you wouldn't normally give. If you're reading this when you should be sleeping, put the book down and GO TO SLEEP.

What if you're still not keeping on top of the behaviour?

If your behaviour management strategies don't seem to be effective enough, now is the time to get a plan in place. If your school leaders are concerned about it, they will have done this already. Talk to your mentor and get a plan set up that will help you move your practice forward and give you the strategies you need. Be open to ideas and try things that you may not have tried before. Take advice from the more experienced members of staff and choose what you think might work for you and for your class.

Give yourself a timescale to try new strategies. Try each one for at least two weeks before reviewing it and commenting on whether it has or hasn't worked. You will know your class and what you think is achievable for them. Keep your expectations high, though!

During the time that you're trying out your plan, ask to observe other teachers using the strategies they have suggested. If possible, get them to teach your class and show you how it's done with your own pupils. A good teacher won't have a problem doing that.

Mistakes

When it comes to coping as an NQT, common mistakes include:

- Not speaking up when you need support. Make sure you talk to someone if you're struggling.

- Trying out a strategy every two minutes. Give things time to work, and you may be pleasantly surprised.

- Ploughing on regardless. If you give a strategy time and it still isn't working, try something else. Don't bury your head in the sand.

- Not giving yourself an honest self-reflection. Nobody is perfect, so make sure you reflect honestly so that you can improve. Feel proud when things go well, and think about what you would do differently should things go wrong.

Action steps

1. Strive to be a better teacher every day. Embrace new learning opportunities and new behaviour management strategies. You'll love this job because you'll never stop learning and your practice will never stop evolving.

2. Keep thinking about the children and what is best for them.

3. If children's behaviour is challenging, look at your style. Think about whether it needs to be adapted to better suit the needs of the class as a whole.

4. Reflect honestly and openly.

5. Seek advice when you need it.

6. Look after your own health and well-being. You'll then be in an excellent place to ensure the behaviour and well-being of your class.

CHAPTER 13

Parting Words

So here we are at the end of our trip together down the road of behaviour management. I truly hope that you are able to take some of the tips that I shared with you and feel confident enough to put them into practice.

Do you know what? Lots of people read books like this and never put anything into place that they have learned. Please do me a favour and write down three things that you think you're going to do when you get ready to meet your new class. Put them into practice and give them time to embed. If they're really not working, reflect on why and see what you could do instead.

As an NQT, you have the opportunity to develop your style from scratch. Think about the style that best suits your personality. Remember to act in the role of a teacher until you feel more confident, if that helps. But be clear on what you want your class's behaviour to look like.

Finally, remember the SIMPLE approach. It will help you to set up consistent systems and clear boundaries that you and the class can work with.

I truly hope that you enjoy your new career as a primary school teacher. The fact that you have read this book shows that you are committed to getting things right for you and for your class.

Thank you

Thank you for joining me on this journey down the winding road of behaviour management. I hope you've found it useful.

If you loved the book and have a moment to spare, I **would be thrilled if you could leave me a short review on the site where you purchased it.** Tell your other NQT friends about it too - your help in spreading the word is greatly appreciated.

If you'd like to receive any more tips and advice during your NQT year (and beyond), please check out my blog at www.thenqtmentor.com.

You can even sign up to receive weekly newsletters via email that will help you with specific aspects of teaching, and are designed to support you through your first year.

I love hearing from my readers, so please do get in contact via the blog or via Twitter and Facebook:

@thenqtmentor

www.facebook.com/thenqtmentor

ABOUT THE AUTHOR

Steph Caswell has been a primary school teacher for over 10 years and has taught across all Key Stages. Since starting her teaching career in 2004, she has been an English subject leader, Key Stage Leader, NQT Mentor, Student Mentor, Assistant Headteacher, Inclusion Leader and, most recently, a Deputy Headteacher.

Steph's website for NQTs, www.thenqtmentor.com helps newly qualified teachers with all aspects of their new career from classroom tips and tricks, to managing difficult conversations with parents. It also aims to provide a community for NQTs to connect with each other and give each other advice on how to cope with the stresses and strains (and successes!) of their first year of teaching.

As well as writing books for teachers, Steph is also available for NQT training within schools and clusters, and for speaking events across the country.

For further information, please check out my 'contact me' page on my website or connect via twitter @thenqtmentor.

Printed in Great Britain
by Amazon.co.uk, Ltd.,
Marston Gate.